What people are saying about …

FAVOR WITH KINGS

"Insightful, humorous, authentic, and relevant, Caleb Anderson gives us a fresh look into an ancient biblical story. Read this book."

Mark Batterson, *New York Times* bestselling author of *The Circle Maker* and lead pastor of National Community Church

"Don't miss out in the life-changing message of this book! Caleb Anderson has an uncanny knack for taking ancient wisdom and making it incredibly practical and relevant. In *Favor with Kings*, he kicks down the door of living an ordinary life to show us how to live and love in extraordinary ways."

Les Parrott, PhD, *New York Times* bestselling author of *Saving Your Marriage Before It Starts*

"*Favor with Kings* is a manifesto that beckons your deepest desires and provides a clear running lane for these God-given dreams to come to life. This journey is not for the faint of heart, but I can promise you that if you're willing to fight on, it will bring out the very best in you."

Steve Carter, teaching pastor at Willow Creek and author of *This Invitational Life*

"Caleb Anderson is an important voice in this next generation, and *Favor with Kings* is an important book. Read it sooner rather than later."

Doug Fields, author, speaker, and consultant

"Caleb Anderson writes *Favor with Kings* in a relevant and challenging way that draws in readers who want to grow and make the most of their lives."

Dennis Gilmore, CEO of First American Title

"I've been a huge fan of Caleb Anderson for about fifteen years now, and if you read this book or spend any time with him, you'll see why! Caleb's pursuit of Jesus has always been challenging to me, and I'm a better man because of it. This book feels more like letters to anyone who wants to practically follow Jesus, and, oh, *change the world*! Thanks, Caleb. Well done."

Tim Timmons, TimTimmonsMusic.com

"Finally! A book that doesn't just inspire or motivate you to greater things, but one that explains how to make them a reality in your life. Caleb writes how he lives: authentically, passionately, and with great purpose!"

Rusty George, lead pastor of Real Life
Church and author of *When You, Then God*

"Caleb Anderson clears the path and gives us clarity and biblical wisdom to reignite our inner passion toward becoming the person God wants us to be! Caleb is a gift to his generation!"

Richard Watts, author of *Fables of Fortune* and *Entitlemania*

"Caleb Anderson is a very gifted leader and writer. He teaches us that God can take our 'mess' and turn it into a 'message' to encourage others. In *Favor with Kings*, Caleb humbly demonstrates how God has given him a message of hope, restoration, leadership, and encouragement."

Chuck Scott, director of development initiatives at Young Life

"This book will surprise you, inspire you, and help you see life differently. Caleb's writing is quick and addictive. You can't stop. And as you go with him on the journey of this book, you will discover that he didn't write it for himself; he wrote it for you."

Hank Fortener, global ambassador for Mosaic and founder of AdoptTogether.org

"Caleb Anderson is the real deal. His life has been shaped by Jesus in the most impactful ways. I have known Caleb through good times and bad and have seen him live out the message of Jesus. His writing is crisp, clear, and refreshing. This book will change you if you let it. Don't just read it; let it work on you. Let the truths settle in and do their work. It's my prayer that all who read this book will be as blessed as I have been by Caleb's ministry."

Dean Curry, senior pastor of
Life Center Tacoma

"'Humility and pain are part of the journey toward becoming the best version of you.' So says Caleb Anderson in *Favor with Kings*. Filled with honesty and fresh insights, Caleb takes us back to the legacy of Nehemiah. This is an encouraging word from a gifted young leader. Read it carefully. It will be good for your soul."

Dr. Larry Anderson, senior pastor
of North Bible Church

FAVOR WITH KINGS

FAVOR WITH KINGS

God's Purpose, Your Passion,
and the Process of Doing Great Things

CALEB ANDERSON

David C Cook®
transforming lives together

FAVOR WITH KINGS
Published by David C Cook
4050 Lee Vance View
Colorado Springs, CO 80918 U.S.A.

David C Cook U.K., Kingsway Communications
Eastbourne, East Sussex BN23 6NT, England

The graphic circle C logo is a registered trademark of David C Cook.

The website addresses recommended throughout this book are offered as a
resource to you. These websites are not intended in any way to be or imply an
endorsement on the part of David C Cook, nor do we vouch for their content.

Bible credits are listed in the back of this book. The author has
added italics to Scripture quotations for emphasis.

LCCN 2016941368
ISBN 978-1-4347-1041-3
eISBN 978-1-4347-1092-5

© 2016 LifeXperiments, LLC
Published in association with Christopher Ferebee, Attorney
and Literary Agent, www.christopherferebee.com.

The Team: Tim Peterson, Keith Jones, Amy Konyndyk,
Nick Lee, Jack Campbell, Susan Murdock
Cover Design: Jon Middel
Cover Photo: Shutterstock

Printed in the United States of America
First Edition 2016

1 2 3 4 5 6 7 8 9 10

062716

*This book is dedicated to the people
who helped it become a reality.*

To:

*Hilary, for your support, encouragement, and
genius insights. You're a brilliant communicator.*

*Kaycee, for committing your work life to
helping me maximize mine. You're a gift.*

*Beth, for blowing up barriers and helping
me blaze trails. You're impressive.*

*Kenton, for your leadership, example, and
for allowing me to be me at Mariners
Church. You're a true mentor.*

Chris, for believing in me and paving the way.

*Tim and team, for your partnership
in the publishing process.*

*The staff and volunteers of Mariners Church
Huntington Beach, for joining me in stacking
stones. You're living a great story.*

I am grateful.

Caleb

CONTENTS

0. Greatness   **13**

1. Memoirs   **19**

2. How Are Things, Really?   **27**

3. Bad News   **37**

4. Hints in Your History   **43**

5. How to Hear from God   **49**

6. Learning in Wait   **57**

7. Cultivating Conviction   **65**

8. All In   **73**

9. Favor with Kings   **81**

10. Excellence   **89**

11. Pray + Plan   **95**

12. When Things Get Real   **103**

13. A Few   **109**

14. See and Learn   **115**

15. Words Create Worlds   **121**

16. The Spark   **131**

17. Blessings and Blood   **137**

18. Stacking Stones   **145**

19. How Things Get Done   **151**

20. Momentum   **157**

21. The Einstein of Delegation   **165**

22. Names   **173**

23. Enemies   **181**

24. Eyes Up   **191**

25. The Good Fight   **199**

26. The Messy Middle   **207**

27. Raise Your Standards   **213**

28. Success and Keeping Your Soul   **219**

29. Persevere   **227**

30. Give It Away   **235**

For Group Discussion   **245**

For Pastors   **275**

Notes   **279**

Bible Credits   **283**

O
_____

GREATNESS

"To accomplish great things, we must not only act, but also dream, not only plan, but also believe." —Anatole France

"Do you want to stand out? Then step down. Be a servant. If you puff yourself up, you'll get the wind knocked out of you. But if you're content to simply be yourself, your life will count for plenty." —Jesus (Matthew 23:11–12 THE MESSAGE)

If you're reading this book because you want to be rich and famous, you'll be disappointed. Disappointed with this book, but also with your life—money and fame don't deliver.

Greatness is real. And possible. But it's not what people sell you.

People will try to make you believe that greatness has something to do with the number of commas in your net worth, the number of bathrooms in your house, or the number of followers you have, socially. It doesn't. We all know people who are successful by these standards and yet, at the same time, are regretful, miserable, and unhappy.

Greatness is more than money, position, or power. It's elusive to many, but also strangely simple to obtain—or, better, to *embrace*.

Greatness is two part:

1. *Intrinsic:* Given by God. You're great because you were created in the image of the God of the universe.[1] Bonus: Because you have God's DNA, you have the creative gene. You have the capacity to create, add value, make better … which brings us to the second part of greatness.
2. *Extrinsic:* Given by others. For something to be great, someone must ascribe value to it. For you to be great, you must add value to the lives of people around you, causing them to be grateful for you. That doesn't mean starting a billion-dollar company—but you might. It doesn't mean writing the next bestseller—but you can. All it really means is that the world is better because you lived, loved, and cared.

If you truly care about the lives of others, they'll be grateful. Gratitude from others suggests that you value *their* intrinsic greatness and that you're having a great impact on the people around you.

Pause for a moment. You may need to reread the sentences above. If you're like me, you're driven, motivated, struggling to stay motivated, and determined to be *somebody*. And you might be going about it all wrong.

Greatness is not about being rich and famous.

Accomplishment is not about bank accounts.

Influence isn't about impressing people.

Don't deceive yourself into achieving for yourself. Greatness is not about what you can accumulate. It's about what you can give away—what you can contribute to the lives of people around you.

Greatness is being your unique, original self and then elevating the unique, God-given value of people around you. And that can play out in an infinite number of ways.

PEOPLE AND PROJECTS

So far, all of this is soft and intangible. And this book is meant to be practical. The way you shift from ethereal to physical is with actual projects that help actual people.

Some people talk a lot about love and service and harmony in the universe but don't actually do anything. Others do a lot, but what they do only seems to benefit their own bottom line. Neither of those paths leads to greatness.

Greatness is in you. But to draw it out, you need to serve someone other than yourself. And, graciously, it turns out that's actually the path to the best kind of life—a life of fulfillment, contentment, and purpose.

Jesus said that the secret to a life of significance is simply to love God by genuinely caring about the people you come into contact with.[2] That includes your home, your work, your school, your energy, your words, your time, your attention, your priorities … in fact, it involves everything.

Love God by loving others.

Become great, personally, by serving other people.[3]

Simple. But not easy.

In this book, I'm going to invite you to work on a project—a project that benefits people. I don't know what that project is. *You* might not yet know what that project is. It doesn't need to be your life's work. But it will at least start you down the path of accomplishing great things.

For the next thirty chapters, I'll invite you to embrace a paradigm: Forget everything you know or think you know about the path to greatness. Open yourself to fresh inspiration from an ancient story of profound influence and accomplishment for the greater good.

Nehemiah's recorded journey dates back to 444 BC, yet its implications can still shape our lives and best efforts today. Allow his story to shed light on your story. Allow his strength to give you strength. And allow his insights and inspiration to spur you on to great things.

And it's my hope that you'll commit to *do something*. Do something that

- you've been moved by;
- you've wondered about but haven't courageously pursued;
- you've started but haven't finished; or
- you're haunted by—something that scares you and speaks to you in your quiet moments.

The pages that follow will help you uncover your mission and clarify your next steps.

Each chapter concludes with a summarizing statement termed "Lesson." After that, I offer an optional "Action" section. The actions are fun, but more than that, they are important. Our American culture subconsciously believes that you learn a lesson when you hear it. That's not true. The reality is that you learn only when you've put the lesson into *practice*. No action, no learning. If you want to learn, grow, change, become, then action is required. There is no substitute.

But if you don't like my action steps, create your own!

I know a workout instructor who works exclusively with out-of-shape individuals who are just starting out on their journey toward health. After I witnessed her coaching a struggling senior citizen who seemed to do only some halfhearted crunches then walk the indoor track before hitting the steam room, I asked her what her objective was with this elderly man. She, in turn, asked me if I knew the "World's Greatest Exercise." Apparently, I didn't, but I wanted to.

Here's the answer: *the one you'll do.*

She starts with whatever exercise the person is willing to do and builds from there.

I offer you the same humble starting point. Start from where you are, and we'll go from there. Who knows … we just might change the world.

Lesson: Greatness is in you, but drawing it out means serving someone else.

Action: Shock someone today—simply by the way you show interest in or serve him or her.

You'll find additional resources for your journey at FavorWithKings.com.

1

———

MEMOIRS

"Uniqueness isn't a virtue. It's a
responsibility." —Mark Batterson

"These are the memoirs of Nehemiah son
of Hacaliah." —Nehemiah 1:1

"These are memoirs of Nehemiah." That means he wrote this story—as it happened, as he saw it, as he participated in it … and for our sake. This is his story, and it will inform your story.

Human stories are always intersecting with and inspiring each other. As Nehemiah opens the pages of his memoirs, I, too, want to give you a glimpse of my unique journey thus far—so that, together, we (Nehemiah, me, and you) might continue to inspire great stories.

SITTING THE BENCH

Heritage Hall sits at the center of the University of Southern California (USC) in Los Angeles. To get to the team meeting room, I had to walk past half a dozen Heisman Trophies and a lot of large, intimidating athletes in workout clothes and headphones. Technically, I was one of them, but I looked small in my own eyes.

I was reporting for my sophomore season on the men's volleyball team, and this was the first team meeting of the new season. We would receive our workout schedule and our new gear, and we would vote on who would represent this international group of giant adolescents as team captain.

At six foot three, I was the second smallest guy on the team. My practice jersey hung off my skinny frame as if I were a twelve-year-old trying on his dad's clothes. I was nineteen and had sat on the bench my entire freshman year. In fact, playing time didn't look good for my sophomore season either. The guy playing in front of me was a twenty-five-year-old junior who would later be invited to play for the US Men's National Team in two Olympics.

Coach passed out the paper and pens. It was the classic write-down-the-name-and-fold routine. We did. I wrote down the name of last year's captain, who happened to be the Olympian playing in front of me. He was a likable guy and a hard worker—and a beast of an athlete. Voting for the incumbent made sense.

The papers were collected, and Coach said something that I don't remember. Then, five minutes later, one of the assistants brought the results to the head coach.

"Well, this is interesting. But I guess it makes sense," Coach said. He was not exactly a master motivator. He continued, "Your 1998–99 team captain is Caleb Anderson."

Really? I barely played. The guy starting in front of me was bigger, faster, and stronger, and he'd been the captain the year prior. How do you lead a team as the smaller, less impressive athlete sitting on the bench?

I remember standing eye to chin with the best volleyball players in the world as I represented the Men of Troy at each pregame coin toss. I'd smile, shake hands, exchange some pleasantries, then walk back to the bench and *not* take off my warm-ups. The other teams probably wondered if I was injured or if the "real" captain was being disciplined. But there I was, unimpressively learning how to influence other people from a place of humility.

That season, I discovered that greatness is often different than we expect; and success can come in a manner we don't anticipate.

I earned the respect of that motley crew of tall athletes not with on-court honors but with character, consistency, and a compelling lifestyle.

Instead of building impressive stats and status as I had planned, the sport of volleyball became about making an impact on my teammates' lives. And fifteen years later, with bad knees and a sad vertical leap, I can say that it's relationships that still count. I've seen teammates show up at the church I lead, I've performed wedding ceremonies, I've given career counsel and relationship advice, and I've had spiritual conversations with half-sober guys in overly honest moments. I've broken up fights, stayed up late talking, and prayed in the middle of a kitchen. It's been an adventure. In fact, looking back, I'd choose this path of second-string humility over being an athletic all-star without hesitation. Stardom lasts for a season. Significance lasts much longer.

HUMILIATION

After graduating from USC, I went to work for Rick Warren (author of *The Purpose Driven Life*), where, at twenty-five, I became the youngest person on his church staff to be licensed as a minister or to speak on the main stage. I moved up the ranks at the large church, learning everything I could. At twenty-six, I left the church to start an organization of my own. That's when my life came undone.

I refer to it as my quarter-life crisis. My first entrepreneurial endeavor never got off the ground. Secretly, I was afraid—afraid of failure and afraid of the pressure I felt to be great. (I wasn't the world's greatest volleyball player, so maybe I could be the world's greatest pastor.) My insecurity and its accompanying coping mechanisms made me difficult to live with and sabotaged my marriage, which ended after a few short years.

At twenty-seven, I was no longer the shiny Golden Boy, and my life was no longer up and to the right. Life and my religious structure were crumbling around me. I questioned everything. Was I a fake? Was God fake? Was I doomed to a life of settling for *oh, well?*

I'll tell you about the silver lining later in the book, but I want you to see that, for me, the path to anything good or significant in my life was paved with pain and humiliation.

Everyone likes humility, but no one wants to be humiliated.

AND THEN THERE'S DEATH

A couple of years later, I remarried. Three months after marrying my beautiful and incredibly fun wife, Hilary, we got the phone call you never want to receive. Her mom, Kimi, had been diagnosed with stage-four pancreatic cancer.

We promptly left everything and moved to Gig Harbor, Washington, to care for my precious mother-in-law in her final weeks. Kimi died. We stayed in Washington. Hilary needed to be around family and to grieve the painful loss.

Talking with Kimi in those final days, watching her family love her well, sitting at her bedside in her final hours—the experience put life in perspective for me. I watched Hilary, a loving daughter, do anything and everything in her power to make her mom laugh, smile, or lie down just a little more comfortably. I saw Hilary's grandparents—Kimi's parents—unable to express their grief, unwilling to give up hope. I saw love at the intersection of life and death, and my lighter and more momentary troubles seemed small.

My view of life became a little clearer, a little simpler. I saw myself more honestly. And I looked at Hilary with more gratitude.

Death leads to life. Animals, plants, seeds, soil, sun—in God's mysterious circle of life, death (evil) is repurposed in service of life (good). The death of one thing drops a seed in fertile soil; the seed takes root and gives life to many other things, which then give life to still more things.

Loss led to gain in my marriage. Pain led to progress in my view of God and the world around me. Kimi will never be forgotten—for many reasons, not the least of which is that her death has birthed life in so many unanticipated ways.

God, and only God, can work all things for good.[4] Even the worst of things.

Nevertheless, pain is pain. And seasons of healing take longer than we want. While we lived in Washington, I struggled. Vocationally, I couldn't get traction. Emotionally, I got the blues from the gray skies. Relationally, I felt like I didn't fit.

Three years into Washington life, my wife came to me and asked, "Do you think we need to move back down to Southern California for you to find more work-related connections?" She knew that the job I was about to accept was just for the money and would kill my soul. And this willingness to uproot from her hometown and extended family was a new, unexpected development.

We moved to Orange County, California, three months later. I had business and entrepreneurial dreams in mind, but shortly after I arrived, a church contacted me. Even though I had the church experience, I wasn't looking for a ministry job—I was avoiding it. I figured I'd tried that, it didn't really work out, and now I should probably apply my USC business education to making some money.

But my wife and I prayed and tried to be open to the possibility of working with Mariners Church in Orange County. Mariners is a great church, and its vision to start and support a network of churches intrigued me.

We said yes to Mariners, but in truth, it felt like we were saying yes to God—as mysterious as that is. A short time later, we found ourselves moving into the center of Huntington Beach and taking

over leadership of a three-year-old Mariners Church that was struggling to find momentum and losing money every month.

Today, we're three years into our journey and we've seen the
church grow exponentially. We're having a quantifiable impact on
the community around us and we're seeing lives changed weekly.
And we're just getting started.

I often stand back in awe and note that I'm watching an act of
God. Me, the reluctant pastor.

NEHEMIAH

At the first church staff meeting I led three years ago, I directed the
team to the book of Nehemiah.

"This is going to be our guiding text for the journey," I told
them. "Not just for today … not just for this year … but for the
journey as we participate with God and lead in building this church."

You can ask anyone on my team about Nehemiah and they will
point you to the principles of this ancient story and how we're apply-
ing them constantly as we engage in the most exciting work any of
us have ever witnessed.

And through this entire journey, here's what *I've* witnessed:
**Humbly embracing the unexpected—unsexy—journey, in service
of others, while building on ancient biblical principles, leads to
*great things***. In fact, this path will propel you to greater accomplishments than you ever believed you'd achieve.

This book is about that. And this book is about *you*.

You have a personal journey unlike anyone else. It might not be
what you expected or what you would have originally chosen, but

it's yours. And you can leverage it—all of it—toward accomplishing something truly great.

You can shift from being self-focused to others-focused.

You can rise out of humiliation and reach toward hope.

You can use pain to discover purpose.

There is greatness in you, and there is something you need to do. But it's not *for you*. It's for someone else. It will require a dose of humility and dedicated intentionality as you

- get to know *yourself*;
- focus on the greater *good*; and
- do something great, with and for *others*.

Lesson: Humility and pain are part of the journey toward becoming the best version of you.

Action: Write down the dream you have for your life but are afraid to talk about out loud—either because it's too big and you don't know how you'll do it or because you fear you've messed it up somehow.

2

HOW ARE THINGS, REALLY?

"Silence becomes cowardice when occasion demands speaking out the whole truth and acting accordingly." —Mahatma Gandhi

"I questioned them about the Jewish remnant that had survived the exile, and also about Jerusalem." —Nehemiah 1:2

You don't know because you don't ask. You don't ask because you don't really want to know.

It was a 1999 Acura TL, and it ran like a dream. Except when you pressed the brake. Then it shook angrily. But how often do you use the brake? Still, I loved that car.

My mom found it at Grandma's retirement community—the best place to buy cars. A sweet old woman was handing over the keys at eighty-nine (thank God). She had only driven the car to church and to the grocery store. I bought it from her when it was ten years old and had just thirty-nine thousand miles on it. Like I said, retirement communities are the best places to buy cars. That is, if you're a frugal-not-flashy consumer who's secure enough to have a Friendship Village decal permanently stuck to your windshield.

As faithful as that '99 Acura was, 2015 felt like the time to let it go. So I did what you do: I got it washed, took pictures (avoiding any shots of paint peeling away from an egg ambush), and posted the pictures on Craigslist. I also had a car-guy friend give it a once-over.

"I don't want to pay to fix anything," I told him, "so please only tell me if I absolutely have to fix something or if I absolutely have to tell the buyer to fix something."

After the first test drive with a prospective buyer, the man made some observations and asked some questions. My answers likely seemed ignorant, and I couldn't argue with his comments. When he offered me $500 less than my asking price, I took it. How could I not? I had chosen to be naive with regard to the true state of the car. I didn't want to know, and it cost me money.

My consequences were minor. My friend Ryan's story has more profound implications.

Ryan grew up in North Fork. It's a small rural town in Northern California that boasts exactly one grocery store and three restaurants. When he was a teenager, Ryan moved to Orange County to live with a family member. The places Ryan lived in Orange County were very different from the places he lived in North Fork. The OC offered an abundance of activities and opportunities that were mind blowing to a kid from a small town. Surfing, skating, Disneyland, supermalls, sparkling movie theaters, and more restaurants than you could visit in a lifetime. Ryan met his wife, had four kids, and earned his living in the OC. But there was a problem. Ryan wondered about North Fork. He couldn't shake the feeling that he had something to offer in a town with so little to offer him. So he used his vacation time to leave the beaches of the OC and take the family on a road trip to North Fork. And everything changed.

To be clear, everything changed for Ryan and his family. Nothing had changed in North Fork. It was rough, run down, and blanketed with the look of *oh, well*.

While they were there, Ryan and his wife asked questions, examined schools, and visited churches. They wanted the answer to one of the most dangerous questions we can ask: "How are things, really?"

By the time they left, Ryan and his wife had a curiously strong sense that North Fork was to be their home.

For the next several weeks, they were restless and irritated by life-as-usual in Orange County. As comfortable as life was, they were uncomfortable in the middle of it. They knew they had to do something.

Just a few months later, they sold half of their belongings and moved into a home in North Fork that could generously be called a fixer-upper. When I asked Ryan how he could leave his beautiful life in Huntington Beach and move to a little town that seemed forgotten, he said, "Because I can't forget it. I just know somewhere down deep inside me that I can't forget that town. In fact, I think I'm supposed to change it."

Today, Ryan has a plan. He has a plan to fix up his house, and he has a plan to make an impact on the town of North Fork.

I think places matter. Ultimately, it's the people in places that matter, but let's just consider *place* for a moment.

I believe there's a place of particular significance to you. It might be a city or county or culture. It might be a workplace, home, or school. It might be geographical, digital, or just theoretical. But I think there's a place out there, somewhere, that matters a little more to you than other places.

Do you have it?

Some of you know exactly what I'm talking about. Your place is clear.

If your place is unclear, start with where you already are. Right here. Believe that you are where you are for a reason. Look around you and notice your place. There's purpose here. It just might require your paying attention. And even if you leave for a different place, the lessons of *this* place will serve you in the next.

And as we consider *place*, let's visualize the following:

- your home
- your neighborhood
- your city or town
- your coffee shop
- your workplace
- your church
- your community center
- your school or your kid's school
- your place of play or recreation

As you visualize these places, look for the people. What are they wearing? What are they doing? How are they feeling?

Is the future bright or bleak? Do you sense faith or fear? Are they thriving or surviving? Do they have what they need, or are their resources scarce? Are they together or isolated?

Now you're on the brink of a difficult decision. Do you sincerely want to know *how are things, really*? Because if you drive to North Fork, if you ask the questions, if you unlock the door to the truth and open your eyes to what's real, there's no going back.

Pause. Sober moment of truth.

And here we go …

JERUSALEM

Nehemiah has a "North Fork." In his memoirs, appropriately titled "Nehemiah," we discover not only his *place* but also his *plans* to bring about monumental change. Nehemiah leads a project so impressive and so important that it has become a model for the ages of what to do when you know you have to do something.

The first chapter of Nehemiah opens in a castle. Nehemiah is not the king—Artaxerxes is—but Nehemiah is in the king's inner circle. The king gives him a chariot with gold rims and pays for his loft in the kingdom. He even brings Nehemiah to all his A-list parties.

We'll talk more about Nehemiah's job in a future chapter, but for now you should know that he's the king's taste tester. He makes sure the food and drink aren't poisoned, and he's also, literally, eating like a king.

And by the way, unlike his king and employer, he's not even Persian. He's Jewish. That means Nehemiah has somehow earned incredible favor with the Persian king, which is especially amazing considering he's eight hundred miles from home and was born a slave in this foreign land.

Approximately ninety years prior, King Nebuchadnezzar was the brutal but brilliant king of Babylon who exploited the weaknesses of the Jewish nation, destroying their capital city of Jerusalem, murdering thousands of people, and capturing Israel's most prized possessions—including the best and brightest young people.

> The king took home to Babylon all the articles, large and small, used in the Temple of God, and the treasures from both the Lord's Temple and from the palace of the king and his officials. Then his army burned the Temple of God, tore down the walls of Jerusalem, burned all the palaces, and completely destroyed everything of value. The few who survived were taken as exiles to Babylon, and they became servants to the king and his sons until the kingdom of Persia came to power.[5]

King Nebuchadnezzar and the Babylon army "tore down the walls of Jerusalem" and burned and destroyed everything of value. (We'll get back to those walls.) And the final phrase of verse 20, "until the kingdom of Persia came to power," indicates that Cyrus, the king of Persia, would later invade and overtake Nebuchadnezzar and Babylon. Cyrus ushered in a new era and was generous to the Jews. He and the Persian kings who followed him allowed thousands of Jews to travel back to Jerusalem to reinhabit their homeland.

After two groups of Jews had returned to Jerusalem and several kings of Persia had died, Artaxerxes took the throne. And that is where we pick up our story.

It would be reasonable to think that, multiple generations removed from the invasion of Nehemiah's ancestors' home, Jerusalem would be a footnote in the story of Nehemiah's life. Sure, he knows of Jerusalem, historically, and he knows that Persia isn't his native land. His father would have instilled in him a respect for his people and his past. Many of his friends and relatives returned to Jerusalem with the Persian king's blessing and an optimistic twinkle in their eyes. But let's be real. He lives in a castle and works directly for a king. It's good to be Nehemiah in Persia.

One day, Nehemiah is sipping fermented grape juice in the west wing and is told that he has visitors. His brother and a few friends made the eight-hundred-mile trek from Jerusalem, and they look terrible. They look terrible not just because they've been walking for three weeks but also because there's a reason they made the journey back to Persia in the first place. Something is wrong.

Upon seeing their faces, Nehemiah's first instinct was probably guilt. "I'm living like the Fresh Prince and my family has fallen on hard times."

Or, perhaps, he could easily have felt used, like a professional athlete with all his clingers-on: "Hey, man, let me be in your entourage. You owe me from that one time … I know you don't think you're better than me now that you have money!"

Imagine you're Nehemiah. You have privilege and opportunities that most do not. Now your family and friends are standing in front of you, and they clearly came here to tell you something serious. What do you do?

Possible options:

- Give them money to go away.
- Take them to a party to get their minds off their troubles.
- Find a more permanent guesthouse and move them back to the kingdom of the Persians.

After all, life is good. Why mess with a good thing? You wouldn't want to screw this up. And you wouldn't want other people making you feel bad that your life is better than theirs. Right?

Right.

However, Nehemiah can't ignore what's standing in front of him. He's unable to dine and drink this reality away. They are his family. His people. From his place. And something isn't right.

It doesn't matter how good or how difficult your life is right now. It doesn't matter how much or how little you have. When God opens your eyes to see a new reality—one that triggers the I-must-do-something instinct—you are haunted until you act.

You can't stick your head in the sand. There's no more distracting yourself with beats and binge watching television. Vegas trips won't satisfy the void that's been exposed in your soul. You're going to have to do something. And the first step is to ask an honest question.

Even though it's more convenient not to know, you must know the truth.

Even though it might mean selling everything and moving to North Fork ...

How are things, really?

Lesson: When your eyes are opened to see reality and injustice, you'll be miserable until you do something.

Action: Fill-in-the-honesty blanks.

When I think of a significant *place*, I think of _____.

When I think of "my *people*," I think of _____.

If I'm honest, I don't care enough about _____.

I think I care about _____,

but I'm distracted by/comfortable with _____.

I want to do something about _____,

so I'm going to _____.

Today, I'm also *not* going to _____

... so that I can pay attention to _____.

3

BAD NEWS

*"Bad news isn't wine. It doesn't improve
with age." —Colin Powell*

*"They said to me, 'Those who survived the exile and are
back in the province are in great trouble and disgrace.
The wall of Jerusalem is broken down, and its gates
have been burned with fire.'" —Nehemiah 1:3*

Bad news is the genesis of breakthroughs.

I'm sure there were some pleasantries exchanged when Nehemiah first greeted his brother and friends, but they didn't last long. There was an elephant in the room.

Nehemiah was living like a king in the palace, and his friends and family just walked eight hundred miles … for a reason. They wore their exhaustion and hopelessness on their faces. And Nehemiah chose to dig in and not ignore the obvious.

Nehemiah: "How are things, really?"

Friends: "Well, it's not good news."

This is how it goes, doesn't it? Your heart sinks, and you think, *Why did I even ask?*

No one likes bad news. No one enjoys tragedy and pain. We know it's a part of life, but we'd all prefer to avoid it as much as possible.

And yet, there is this strange idea called *compassion*. It's the essence of care and concern and being willing to help when possible.

Compassion is one of the purest expressions of humanity.

Compassion is Mother Teresa giving her life to serve the poor. It's the family who goes to mind-boggling lengths to adopt the child who wouldn't otherwise have a future. Compassion is the meal with the homeless person. It's pulling over and helping push the car off the road. Compassion is sitting in stillness and crying with the friend who's suffered great loss, because words are inadequate.

Compassion is asking, identifying, and doing what you can.

Nehemiah has compassion for his people, and they see that, so they tell him the bad news. And it is bad news.

Not only has Jerusalem—a city once famous for its strength and God's blessings—been reduced to ash and rubble, but no one has been able to do anything about it. The temple was rebuilt, but when the people attempted to rebuild the city and its walls, great opposition mounted, the Persian king intervened, and the project was stopped.[6] The Jews found themselves stuck. Once optimistic, they had become frustrated. Once inspired, they had given up hope.

There's a psychological principle we see in institutionalized inmates called "prisonization" that suggests that people who view themselves as prisoners (degenerates, victims, etc.) will continue to act in alignment with that perception even if their circumstances change. In this case, it's likely that even though the Jewish captives were freed and returned home, they still viewed themselves as insignificant, hopeless, and unworthy or incapable of meaningful progress. In other words, they were still acting like powerless slaves.

That psychological battle persists as one of the great human struggles. We live in alignment with our beliefs. We act in accordance with how we see ourselves. And most of us have a small or negative view of ourselves.

Nehemiah listens to the description of broken-down walls and gates burned by fire, but he can see through the words to a deeper reality. He sees a people who lost their identity, lost their strength, and were barely clinging to some shred of hope—*maybe Nehemiah can influence the king.*

As Nehemiah looks at his friends, he sees past the surface of the issues. As he hears the report, he *listens* at a deep level.

Sure enough, it was bad news. But that bad news was about to change everything.

PURPOSE FROM PAIN

At twenty-eight years old, Justin led an office of commercial-lending salespeople and made a lot of money. He and his wife, Danielle, were overachievers and living the dream—beautiful home, nice cars, luxurious vacations. And then …

Boom. Pregnant. The greatest blessing on top of all their other blessings. They were ecstatic.

Halfway into the pregnancy, however, Justin and Danielle received bad news. Their precious boy was growing without kidneys. He wouldn't survive.

And just like that, everything changed.

Hudson James was induced prematurely so his doting parents could meet him, hold him, kiss him, and cherish him. He lived one hour.

That one hour, and that one little boy, changed Justin's and Danielle's lives forever.

They started the Hudson James Foundation, through which they provide scholarships to Justin's alma mater and have helped build the children's facility at Mariners Church in Huntington Beach. Justin left his job and started his own company so he could ensure that the work he was engaged in would be done ethically and that both employees and customers would be treated with respect.

Justin and I regularly have conversations about refusing to settle in life, doing what matters most, and honoring God by loving people and making the most of the gifts we've been given. And Hudson James still provides inspiration.

I'll never forget crying with Justin and Danielle when they received the bad news. I'll never forget the balloons rising high above the beach at the memorial service for Hudson James. And I'll never forget the lasting legacy that Hudson and his parents are leaving in this world— turning the deepest of pain into purpose for life.

What bad news have you received? What is your deep pain? Is there an ache in your soul? You may have moved on and dealt with it in a healthy way, but pain still shapes our experience of life.

And pain, if dealt with honestly, will lead us to our greatest passions.[7]

Maybe you know immediately what your great pain is. Maybe there are too many to choose from. Or perhaps you've been spared tragedy up to this point in your life. But pain is inevitable.

I recently heard a comedian talk about the pain she'd lived through. She said that pain will always sting but that she's decided to view pain as a gift—it gives her great material!

That's one way of looking at it. Here's an even better way: **God doesn't waste pain.** In fact, pain is often the catalyst for the greatest contributions.

Pain might be telling you something. Have you been listening? Are you leveraging the pain of your past for the sake of progress?

Maggie and Beth talked to numerous young women in our church and listened to their concerns and insecurities around not knowing how to cook. They promptly started a group that met in their kitchens and began teaching younger moms how to make meals for their growing, busy families on a budget.

Blake Mycoskie started TOMS Shoes after traveling to Argentina and seeing children running the streets with bare feet. Realizing this was a global poverty issue and believing that he had the capacity to do something about it, Blake pioneered the now famous business model called One for One—you purchase one pair of shoes, and his organization gives another pair to a child in need.

C. S. Lewis said, "God whispers to us in our pleasures, speaks in our conscience, but shouts in our pains: it is His megaphone to rouse a deaf world."

What about you? What breaks your heart? Have you heard God shout? Is there bad news that lingers, compelling you to do something?

Remember, your *doing* something is part of this process. It doesn't have to be "big." The size and scope of your project doesn't matter. What matters is that you follow the path and leverage the principles laid out in Nehemiah.

Read and you forget. See and you understand. *Do* and you make a difference.

Your project might become a for-profit company, a nonprofit organization, a ministry of a church, a community-engagement opportunity, a corporate Skunk Works effort, a weekend activity, an online campaign, a social movement, or any number of things. The possibilities are endless.

Choose to do work that matters. Ask the question, *How are things, really?* Allow bad news to spark good works.

It's time.

Lesson: God doesn't waste your pain.

Action: Define the bad news that might be pointing you toward purpose. Research the issue that stands out.

What are the facts?

Who are the players?

Where are the biggest needs and opportunities?

How do your assets and abilities align with the needs?

Take notes. Look for bright spots. Listen for direction. Do more than search the Internet. Interview people who might shed light on the issue you're wrestling with. Find people who are already doing similar things, and learn from them.

4

HINTS IN YOUR
HISTORY

"I'm from Akron, Ohio." —LeBron James

"Hanani, one of my brothers, came from Judah." —Nehemiah 1:2

Clues about your future are hidden in your past.

Nobody living outside of Miami, Florida, liked how LeBron James made his decision to take his talents to South Beach. But everybody outside of Miami respected the day he went home. In his words:

> Before anyone ever cared where I would play bas-
> ketball, I was a kid from Northeast Ohio. It's where
> I walked. It's where I ran. It's where I cried. It's
> where I bled. It holds a special place in my heart.
> People there have seen me grow up. I sometimes

feel like I'm their son. Their passion can be overwhelming. But it drives me. I want to give them
hope when I can. I want to inspire them when I
can. My relationship with Northeast Ohio is bigger
than basketball. I didn't realize that four years ago.
I do now.[8]

Where you come from matters.

You might be trying to forget the past, but you can't afford to. It's
too important to your future.

My grandfather was a preacher, traveling around the southwest-
ern United States in an RV, sometimes being paid in large sacks of
beans. Literally. My father spent thirty years working for a nonprofit,
faith-based organization called Young Life that served high school
and junior high school students. At sixteen years old, I developed
a feeling—a sense or spiritual intuition—that I, too, would go the
way of my family and become a preacher. But that can mean a lot of
things, right?

During my senior year at the University of Southern California,
I was finishing an expensive undergraduate degree in business—
business communication emphasis—and I liked the idea of going
into the real world and making lots of money using my speaking and
writing skills. The whole "preacher" thing was off my radar. Until the
fateful week I was about to sign on with a company in downtown LA
but received an invitation to work for a church instead.

Really, a church? I thought. I didn't much connect with the
churches I had gone to as a kid, and I knew I was designed differently from my preacher grandpa. Yet I couldn't shake the sense that,

perhaps, this was a divine detour. It reminded me of the sense or impression I had experienced when I was sixteen.

There are clues about your future hidden in your past.

Today I find myself leading a church in Huntington Beach, California. I wasn't sure this was for me, but I love what I get to do, and I love the people I'm privileged to serve. We will soon take over an old movie theater, and my business savvy has come in handy throughout the process. I also help lead an expanding network of churches—the Rooted Network—while writing books. Turns out I'm a preacher-writer-entrepreneur. Thanks, Grandpa. Thanks, USC.

CUPBEARER TO THE KING

Consider Nehemiah. He was a Jewish guy living in a Persian palace. We don't know what he did to climb this ladder of opportunity, but he was there. He was liked. He was trusted.

So trusted, in fact, that the Persian king placed his own life in Nehemiah's hands every day. Nehemiah's job was to taste test anything and everything put on a fancy plate in front of his royal highness. Steak and shrimp? Don't mind if I do. Thousand-dollar bottle of wine? I sip first, King.

Nehemiah was in a position of privilege and prominence, literally eating at the king's table.

Favor has a future. If you're in a place of influence, it's not for you. You have the influence you have for the sake of others. It's never just about you.

For Nehemiah, his successful ascent in the palace would lead to an opportunity he never imagined: an opportunity that would

change his life, his friends' and family's lives, and the lives of countless people to follow.

FOR SUCH A TIME AS THIS

There is another ancient Hebrew story that has been passed down
for generations and is regarded as one of the great stories of divine
destiny. It took place in the same general time period in history as
Nehemiah's.

The Persian king Xerxes (predecessor to Artaxerxes in Nehemiah)
rejected his wife for her disrespectful behavior, and in an effort to
satisfy himself, he ordered the most beautiful women in the area to
come to the palace and be his harem. There were months of beautification treatments provided for these already-gorgeous women—he
was the king, after all.

But of all the women brought to the palace and put in front of
the king, one woman stood out: Esther. Not only did she win the
admiration of the palace staff, but she immediately became the king's
favorite, and he ultimately made Esther his wife. A Jewish girl in a
Persian palace, from the other side of the tracks. But beauty is in the
eye of the beholder, and King Xerxes loved Esther more than any
other woman.[9]

The story doesn't end there. Not long after Esther is honored and
elevated by the king, a controversy breaks out in the kingdom surrounding her people, the Jews. There is a subtle plot with the seeds
of genocide that gains traction and threatens the lives of every Jewish
person in the Persian kingdom. Esther's relative writes her from outside the palace and tells her of the severity of the plot and begs her

to use her influence to help the king see the situation for what it is—and to spare their lives. The danger for the Jews is real, but the immediate danger for Esther is even greater. If she goes before the king and he is in a bad mood or disagrees with her, she will forfeit all her favor and risk being put to death on the spot. (Apparently, that's how kings would operate to exert control over their environments.) Aware of the risks involved, this is the message that came back from Esther's relative:

> He sent back this answer: "Do not think that because you are in the king's house you alone of all the Jews will escape.... And who knows but that you have come to your royal position for such a time as this?"[10]

For such a time as this.

Not only did Esther risk everything, influence the king, and save her people, but her bold example would have a direct influence on the next king to sit on that throne and be served wine by Nehemiah: Artaxerxes. One story builds upon the next.

Your story is building upon the stories and work of others. You will stand on their shoulders. In the future, others will stand on yours.

Today, you, too, have come to your position, your passion, your opportunity … for such a time as this. And what if it's bigger than you think? What if the implications of your actions go further than you realize? What if the idea, burden, or awareness that now haunts you has implications for more than just you?

And what if there are hints in your history that are telling you so?

ONE OF MY BROTHERS

Nehemiah was looking in the face of his brother. Family. Being friends with the king is one thing, but family is something else. Something deeper.

Nehemiah knew who he was and where he was from. He also was beginning to realize that he'd come to his position—cupbearer in the inner circle of the king—for such a time as this.

Lesson: Your past is telling you something about your future.

Action: Consider how your past journey is leading you to your next journey. Fill in the spaces:

> Where I come from:
> Where I want to go:
>
> Who has mattered to me:
> What has shaped me:

Words, shapes, pictures, symbols from my journey:

What "for such a time as this" might mean for me:

5

HOW TO HEAR
FROM GOD

"Why is it that when we speak to God we are said
to be praying but when God speaks to us we are
said to be schizophrenic?" —Lily Tomlin

"When I heard these things, I sat down and wept.
For some days I mourned and fasted and prayed
before the God of heaven." —Nehemiah 1:4

In most cases, we don't listen until we're desperate.

God is all around us—all the time, in everything. But we busy ourselves with a flurry of activities and fill our minds with meaningless chatter. Our lives are saturated with noise, and the volume of competing voices drowns out whatever still, small messages might be whispered our way.

What if when you prayed, you didn't just talk but you also listened? What if when you listened, you heard something? What if when you heard something, it changed everything?

It did for Nehemiah.

We don't read anything about Nehemiah hearing God's audible voice. But we do see in chapter 1 of Nehemiah's memoirs that by the time he finishes his prayer, he has a clear sense of what he needs to do next.

From my experience, this is often how God speaks. There are subtle promptings when I'm paying attention. There is pain when I'm not. And there are circumstances I see, senses I feel, and indications pointing me in a direction until the totality of the information suggests a message of some kind, and I just know that this must be what God is saying.

A BOLD MOVE

I told you that when Hilary's mom got sick we promptly moved to Washington State and stayed there three years after her mom's passing. I love my wife. And I loved my mother-in-law. And there were definitely positive things about living in the Northwest. But I was restless. I had the sense that it just wasn't for me.

While I was struggling to get my feet under me and build financial stability in that new town, Hilary was growing frustrated. She was making more money than I was and working hard to do so. She expressed to me her frustration and suggested I simply take a "normal job" that paid decent money instead of dabbling in experiments that weren't paying off. I could feel a small part of me starting to die.

There's a tension here. I felt a noble obligation to provide for my family. Hilary wanted to have kids and didn't want to keep running at that pace. At the same time, I had dreams, ideas, and projects that I wanted to try. The problem was, nothing was happening fast enough—nothing was coming to fruition. I was unclear where I should focus my efforts and resources. I was floundering. And I was getting closer and closer to taking a "normal job," even though it felt like cutting off my right arm.

One night, Hilary was at a Bible study, and some girlfriends inquired about life and how she was doing. Hilary talked about our dilemma and expressed frustration about my slow progress and resistance to selling out to the paycheck. The girls nodded, more or less understanding. Then they prayed. One of the girls prayed specifically for Hilary. She prayed that God would help Hilary support me and believe in me and that there would be some kind of breakthrough.

Hilary was livid.

With her eyes closed and head bowed, she thought, *I have been supporting. Now is the time when he supports me and makes some money!* I'm paraphrasing her inner, midprayer thoughts on the matter.

And yet, the next morning, something new was residing in Hilary's mind. A new prompting was prodding her spirit.

Before I left the house, Hilary hugged me, looked in my face, and said, "If you think we need to move back down to Orange County for you to find work that's meaningful to you, I'm willing to do that." She couldn't believe the words had come out of her mouth. What was even more staggering was that she realized she meant them.

"Are you serious?"

"Yes, I'm serious."

There was one condition. I needed to find a job that covered our expenses prior to our move. So I flew down to California the next week.

Later the same day we had our conversation, Hilary went to see her grandma—her mom's mom. She asked her grandma what she thought was the right thing to do. Without hesitation, her grandma said, "You do whatever you need to do to support your husband, dear. We'll be okay up here." Hilary cried. The message was becoming clearer.

Two weeks later, I was offered a job. It wasn't much, but it was enough to make the jump. And we did. By that time, the message was loud enough and clear enough to both of us that we made the move.

Since we heard that message and followed that leading, I can't begin to tell you how obvious the path has become. Countless doors have opened, connections have been made, needs have been met, and blessings have been poured out. Hilary misses her family, but she has never doubted that we heard from God, and she is grateful that we listened.

I want to take this a bit further and offer you a few more specific and practical ways you can pay attention and hear from God.

GUT CHECK

Instincts matter. God gave you an inner consciousness. It speaks to you about situations you should flee, people you should avoid, temptations that will hurt you, and opportunities you should run toward. Your voice of conscience is a divine, spiritual mechanism of awareness and discernment. The common term people give this inner awareness or instinct is *gut*.

Your gut is like an inner-instinctual-discernment reflex, and it is in you for a reason. Trust it. And train it by measuring its tugs against reference points you already depend on as *truth*.[11]

PEACE

The Scriptures use a term for *peace* called *shalom*. It's more than the lack of war. The word means "wholeness, harmony, completeness, connectedness." Shalom is your future. One day, you'll experience this harmonious connectedness in every sense with every living thing. In the meantime, your lack of peace is an indicator—like a flashing light or siren—letting you know that shalom is broken.

If you can't sleep, something is wrong. You didn't need me to tell you that, but what's become "normal" might be misleading you. Drugs, TV, alcohol, and other relaxant resources are masking a bigger problem. The cause may be any number of things—pain from the past, shame about your secrets, anxiety about your future. But at its essence, a lack of peace is a reflection of disconnectedness from God, others, and self.

AGREEMENT

Nehemiah prays in agreement with promises God has previously made. He is reminding God of these promises and aligning his plans with what seem to be God's purposes.

In chapter 1, verses 5–9, Nehemiah prays a prayer of reminder.

"God, you promised …"

"God, you said …"

"God, now is the time, these are the days, we are your people …"

The Scriptures are full of principles for progress, stories of encouragement, examples of God's nature, and *promises*. When you pray, pray in alignment with what God has already said. Focus especially on the words of Jesus.[12]

WISDOM FROM OTHERS

A lot of smart people lack wisdom. You see it everywhere—bright, capable, successful people doing idiotic things that destroy their lives. Unwise.

Many think that wisdom is gained by experience. Not true. Wisdom is gained by *learning* from experiences. But there's more …

The highest form of wisdom is learning from the experiences of others. Think of all the pain you would have avoided if you had learned from the experiences of others instead of going down those roads yourself!

"The way of fools seems right to them, but the wise listen to advice."[13]

We've already discussed another way that you can hear from God—through your own story. Look back to go forward. There are clues in your past that point toward your future. After that, then:

- Check your gut.
- Test your experience of peace.
- Align with things God has already said.

- Invite the wisdom of others.
- And, as Nehemiah did, *pray*!

If you do, you'll not only hear from God, you'll be on your way to making the next right decision.

And in the event that you're still just not 100 percent sure whether you're hearing from God, fall back on this simple standard: *look for God's guidance, then choose a path you can embrace wholeheartedly.*

Sometimes you'll be confident in divine direction. At other times, you'll feel it's a crapshoot. Either way, it's only you who can choose. And you must.

Choose the path you feel …

Choose the path you think …

Choose the path that's choosing you.

Lesson: God still speaks, and you can hear him.

Action: Consider how God might be speaking to you through any or all of these avenues. Set aside time to be still, listen, and record what you might be hearing.

Pain from my past (What does my story or journey tell me?):

My gut instincts (What do I already know?):

Peace in the process (What does restlessness, discontentment, or the opposite suggest?):

Agreement with God (What has God already said about my dilemma, and how can I best align?):

Wisdom from others (Who are people I can talk to about my next steps? List them below.):

_____

_____

_____

6

LEARNING IN WAIT

"We learn by example and by direct experience because there are real limits to the adequacy of verbal instruction." —*Malcolm Gladwell,* Blink

"I was cupbearer to the king." —*Nehemiah 1:11*

We don't know how long Nehemiah worked for Artaxerxes, but we know it was long enough to earn the king's complete trust. You've never been king of Persia, but let me tell you, it's got more perks and more pressures than you can imagine. When you're the king, everyone wants something. Everyone has an agenda. And a lot of people's agenda is your death. Guards are stationed at your side constantly. An army protects the castle and advances the cause. And there is someone taste testing everything you put in your mouth to ensure it hasn't been tampered with.

Cupbearer—taste tester—that was Nehemiah's job. It's a good gig, until it's not.

Imagine daily looking into the eyes of a man putting his life on the line with every sip, making sure it is his health and not yours at risk. You can see how a sense of trust and loyalty would begin to build. In honest moments, you realize that no one really cares about your staying alive. They just prefer the idea that their king not be assassinated. Murdered kings have a way of bringing doubt and instability to the kingdom.

Bear in mind that Xerxes, Artaxerxes's father, was murdered in his own bedroom. A king's mortality and the haunting awareness that one has enemies were very much in Artaxerxes's consciousness. You think he was selective about who he let in? Yes, he was. And Nehemiah—the loyal cupbearer Jew—was in.

Now turn your mind to what it meant to be *in*. How many times do you grab a water bottle, tea, or cup of coffee in a day? How often do you eat? Three meals? Plus a snack? The health conscious among us know that what's healthiest for the metabolism is eating smaller, more frequent meals. (Some of my serious fitness friends eat six times a day.) We don't have a precise menu of Artaxerxes's meal plans, but we know he was the king. He got whatever he wanted whenever he wanted it. He had the best food available and the best information available about food. It is my guess that he ate continuously—more than three sit-down meals a day. Which means that Nehemiah was constantly in his presence.

And what do you do when you're stressed? You eat. You think that's a new thing Americans came up with? Nope. Artaxerxes had the same habit. And when are you stressed? When you have significant decisions to make. The king had such decisions as what to do about a revolt against his authority in Egypt and how to strategically finance the enemies of his enemies. Certainly Nehemiah listened as Artaxerxes processed whom he would put in key positions in his kingdom and military and why. No doubt Nehemiah noted how Artaxerxes mobilized and motivated the people under him toward significant efforts. Nehemiah was there. He saw it. He heard the insider chatter. He watched the drama of dilemmas take shape. And he learned.

Nehemiah watched, listened, and learned while he waited for whatever his future might hold.

Before we go any further, it's important to point out that your next right action may well be to *wait*.

But there are two kinds of waiting. Intentional waiting is strategic and purposeful. Passive waiting is just wasting time. Passive waiting is scared stalling. You know there is something for you to do, but you don't do it. There is a sacrifice to make, but you won't make it. There is someone in need, but you're slow to serve. There is some new endeavor or project, but you're not willing to take the risk and jump.

Intentional waiting is different. Sometimes the timing isn't right. There are things that need to fall into place before the project can launch. So you watch and wait on:

- the season of the year
- the financial resources
- the support of a spouse
- the right partner or plan

But you can't afford to *just* wait.

Prepare while you wait.

Jim grew up on a farm in Idaho. With limited opportunities and very few resources, he began working for a new network marketing company in the late 1950s. He was mentored by the founders of the company and became quite successful. Though the company soon went out of business, Jim was asked to speak at his Rotary Club and then to several small groups of businesspeople interested in his passion for life and his methods of personal development.

In 1963, Jim offered his first seminar at the Beverly Hills Hotel. He would go on to present workshops on his personal development philosophy for more than forty years all over the world.

You might not have heard of Jim Rohn, but you've heard of the young man who studied under him before becoming the world's most famous life coach—Tony Robbins.

At seventeen, Tony had no mentors, a broken family, and little direction for his life. He sought out Jim Rohn and offered to work for him—*for free*—just to be in his sphere of influence. Tony hustled and worked himself into a meaningful role. He learned everything he could from Jim before striking out on his own.

To this day, Tony Robbins points to the late Jim Rohn as his primary mentor—in life and in the personal development business. He credits Jim for teaching him that "happiness and success in life are not the result of what we have, but rather of how we live and what we do with the things we have."[14]

It's worth noting that Jim Rohn was a man of faith. He wove spiritual and scriptural truths into his work, leaving a legacy far beyond dollars—influencing the hearts and souls of his protégés and pupils.

Tony Robbins has said, "If you want to be successful, find some-one who has achieved the results you want and copy what they do and you'll achieve the same results."

You and Tony Robbins might have different definitions of "suc-cess," but that doesn't mean there isn't truth (and genius) in the principle.

Mentors accelerate your learning curve. Role models save you time and trouble.

While I was working for Rick Warren at Saddleback Church, he hired a man named David. When David arrived, it was the first time I'd ever heard of him. He came from a different town, where he was in law enforcement, and apparently he came because he felt called by God to work for Rick.

I later learned that his "call" to work for Rick was a sense he had experienced years prior. He had written a letter to Rick saying, "I feel like I'm supposed to come and work for you and your church, but my wife and family are not yet ready to make this kind of transition."

Rick promptly responded (I'm paraphrasing), "Then wait. Don't do it. You need your family on board. In the meantime, pray and prepare. I'm sure we'll talk again one day."

David waited. He attended Rick's conferences. He read his books. He prayed—for Rick and for his own family's journey. Then it happened. A position at Saddleback opened at the exact time David's wife said she was ready and believed God was in the transition. So they leaped.

For the past ten years, David has been the chief of staff for Saddleback Church and essentially runs Rick's life. He's the gatekeeper, relationship manager, and right-hand man. Rick relies on David, and David and his family have become part of Rick's family.

It happened because David waited. And while he waited, he prepared … for such a time as this.

WEALTH IN WISDOM

What are we learning while we wait? In a word, *wisdom*. But more specifically:

- Principles: things that are usually true, regardless of person, setting, or industry.
- Practices: ways of operating that are better than other ways.
- Pitfalls: decisions and directions to avoid.

While you're waiting, glean the principles, study the best practices, and note the pitfalls.

In our world of start-ups, church plants, and Internet sensations, few are willing to prepare while they wait. There are some things you can learn only by doing, but wisdom learns from the experience of others.[15]

In ancient Jewish terms, intentional mentorship was called "following in the dust of the rabbi." The idea was that students would dedicate themselves to following so closely behind a mentor-teacher that they would literally be covered in their teacher's dust. Listening to every word. Watching every action. Modeling. And *waiting*. Waiting for the day when they would go their own way.

Personally, I was blessed with parents whose example I could proudly follow. With a firm foundation, I studied business while playing volleyball at USC. Though I anticipated working in the private sector out of college, I followed an internal prompting to work for Rick Warren at Saddleback Church. I listened to everything Rick said. I read everything he wrote. I learned … I waited.

When I took over leadership of a church, it was not the first time I had led a team or organization. But it was the first time I needed to lead while also preparing sermons every Sunday. That's intense, by the way. Standing up in front of a lot of people—multiple times a Sunday—delivering a message that is expected to be inspiring, funny, relevant, authentic—oh, and *from God*. No pressure.

Fortunately, I could rely on excellent models. I met weekly with Kenton Beshore—senior pastor of Mariners Church in Irvine. On top of that, my dad is now a pastor, as was his father before him, and I listen to other great leaders and teachers via podcasts. Wisdom is within your reach. Listen for it. Seek it out. Ask for it.[16]

Someone out there knows exactly what you need to prepare you for what's next. Find that person.

Lesson: Waiting is for preparing.

Action: List your mentors.

    Mentor I'm watching in person: _____

    Mentor I'm watching from afar: _____

    Mentor I'm listening to (podcast): _____

    Mentor I'm reading: _____

Don't waste waiting. Watch. Listen. Learn. Who's the best at what you want to do, and how can you learn from that person's example?

7

CULTIVATING CONVICTION

"The people that make the biggest impact in the world are the people with the strongest convictions." —Rick Warren

"I mourned and fasted and prayed before the God of heaven. Then I ..." —Nehemiah 1:4–5

Cling to your convictions. Abandon your assumptions.

Assumptions suppose. Convictions *believe*.

My friend Jimmy went to a junior college until his grades were good enough to transfer to USC, whose school and football program he'd been obsessed with his entire life. He volunteered for the football team—ball boy, water boy, whipping boy—it didn't matter what he had to do, he just wanted to be part of the action. Like a Trojan "Rudy" who would never put on pads, Jimmy had a dream to be part of the team, one of the guys. And he did it. In fact, he still does it. He drives up from San Diego to Los Angeles to tailgate and go to games during football season. He's borderline obsessed.

He has conviction.

"This is my team. I've always loved them. I'll always love them."

But Jimmy has more important convictions that go beyond football. Four years ago, he and his wife, Roilyn, sensed a spark in their souls toward adoption.

Jimmy believes that every life matters, that every kid deserves a chance. And that conviction led him to the belief that one of his family's great contributions to the world would be raising one or more adopted children who needed a home and a future.

Six-year-old Chase was born addicted to meth and Vicodin. His birth mother smoked heavily during pregnancy. At four months, Chase was severely shaken and left to die until a babysitter noticed something was wrong and called 911. The doctors cut his skull open to relieve the pressure in his brain and gave him a 10 percent chance of survival. Chase was a fighter and pulled through. And after he spent a year in foster care, Jimmy and Roilyn adopted Chase as their son.

They had never been parents before—not even to a healthy child, let alone a child with severe complications. But it was a non-issue to Jimmy. I remember him telling me, "This is crazy. I realize that I have no idea how hard this is going to be. But this little guy needs us. I'm going to be his dad, and we're going to love him well as long as he lives."

Chase has endured another brain surgery, multiple diseases, and countless therapy sessions. When a child has had such severe setbacks to deal with, you can imagine the roller coaster of emotions, behavior fluctuations, health issues, financial costs, and "why did we do this?" moments. But Jimmy and Roilyn never looked back, never quit, and never stopped loving little Chase. Today, Chase is a smart, stubborn, funny miracle boy, shattering every modest expectation for his life. Chase has a chance. He has a future. And he is well loved.

All of this because of a conviction: "Every child matters." And that conviction inspired Jimmy and Roilyn not just to adopt, but to adopt a child with serious trauma. And the conviction still inspires them to go to any lengths necessary to care for their precious son.

WHY

In recent years, Simon Sinek has shed light on a fundamental human motivation. We are less compelled by "what" and more inspired by "why."[17] The thing itself is less important than *why* the thing exists. One guy's product is cool, but hers will win the day because of her *why* story—the inspiration and genesis behind her effort to create the product in the first place.

Why is what compels us. We are creatures led by our hearts. Our heads work out the details, but our hearts lead the way.

What you believe will determine how you behave. *Why* you take action will inform *how* you proceed, *what* you deliver, and whether you'll stick with it through the struggle.

Perhaps your work feels more like an assignment, not a calling. Maybe you've been asked to do something and you're not sure it aligns with your personal ideas about the future. Or perhaps you know you need to make a change; you just don't have the courage to leap.

You need stronger convictions.

Luckily for you, *convictions can be cultivated.*

Nehemiah cultivated and deepened his convictions. We read that after he received the bad news of Jerusalem's destruction, he threw himself into a period of prayer and fasting. When you're fasting, it's not a just-a-few-hours kind of thing. That's called a late dinner. Fasting is a several-days-or-even-weeks kind of thing. Nehemiah spent time focusing and restricting his comforts in an effort to eliminate distractions so that he could hear from God and determine what he should do next.

Nehemiah felt sadness over the news of his family and the Jewish people in Jerusalem as soon as he heard the report. But you don't put your life on the line for sadness. It takes a bigger why.

Nehemiah needed deeper convictions before he took his leap of faith.

AN INVITATION

My first marriage ended in divorce when I was twenty-seven years old. In retrospect, it was my fault, my failures, and my pride that can be blamed, but I was shocked at the time.

I remember the pain. The first time I saw the closet half empty, I lay down on the ground and cried for a day and a half. The loss of my marriage was the most pain I'd experienced. To make matters worse, the embarrassment, judgment, and rejection from "friends," mainly religious people, were lemon juice in an open wound.

The years that followed were marked by healing, reflecting, learning to believe again, and learning to be me—a more real version of me. More authentically faithful and less judgmental, I learned to trust God and other people again, but I had fewer have-tos and shoulds, and very little religious scaffolding around my life.

Life was more fluid and free. Grace and truth were interwoven, not competing. Life was beauty and gratitude. I didn't have time for pressure-induced performance or looking the part. In a way, I was beginning again. And it was good.

Imagine my surprise when, seven years later, I sensed God moving me to embrace an invitation to lead a church in Huntington Beach. The opportunity wasn't in my five-year plan, nor would it have been on my dream board (if I had had one). In fact, a big part of me wanted to run the other way. I'd experienced enough judgment at the hands of the devout. Certainly I would again disappoint the critical.

And what of Huntington Beach? Sure, it was a beach town in Orange County, but I knew nothing of it. I'd been there for the Fourth of July, but it wasn't a place I'd dreamed about or circled on a map.

Nevertheless, I had a feeling. And an invitation.

I used to think that God had one plan for my life. Oh, and by the way, I've screwed it up … a thousand times. But fortunately, God's *one plan* has multiple iterations.

It's a mystery, but God's plan seems to be laced with elastic—allowing for my stumbles, detours, and distractions. What was bad and could have gotten even worse, God leveraged for a purposeful, positive outcome. Who knows what would have happened if I had been the world's greatest husband from day one; but what I know is that I'm more grateful, graceful, and careful today. Turns out, I'm also more relatable, useful, and humble—making me a far more effective pastor, speaker, and writer.

Hilary and I accepted the opportunity to lead Mariners Church in Huntington Beach. I read the story of Nehemiah, and I concluded that when he fasted and prayed, God gave him more and more *conviction* about his hurting friends and family in Jerusalem. Not only that, but I believe God gave clarity to Nehemiah about one action that would be a multiplier of great impact. Rebuilding the broken-down wall that surrounded the city was not just about a wall—it was about a new start.

Sometimes one intentional action leads to a variety of positive outcomes. You might have been stuck at every turn yesterday. But one simple tweak today might throw open multiple doors that were previously barricaded.

As a result of my meditating on Nehemiah, I decided to fast and pray. I walked the streets and beaches of Huntington, inviting God to increase my conviction for the people in the community. I made introductions, asked questions, listened, and learned. In a short amount of time, I knew this was my path.

And I found that after I committed to the path, new passion filled my heart.

Feelings follow actions. Even if you don't *feel* it first, when you believe it and decide it, feelings will follow.

It's similar to being in love. If you live only by what you feel, you'll get married in a month and divorced in a year. If you learn that you can make choices that cultivate emotions, you'll have the best marriage around.

Here are a few things that I've discovered cultivate strong convictions:

1. **Hang around people with strong convictions.** Conviction, like energy, is contagious. The more you're around deep convictions, the stronger your own certainty and clarity will become.

2. **Deepen your understanding of the realities for real people living actual lives.** The more you know, the more you need to do something about it. When the people have faces (and are not just statistics), it triggers genuine compassion. When cities have personalities, you care. When organizations embody a bigger story of teamwork and collective compassion, you'll be moved to make a difference.

3. **Develop a morning ritual.** Your day will go better if you begin with intention, clarity, and purpose. Focus every morning on what matters most.[18] You can print a free PDF of my daily scheduling tool and personal daily rituals at FavorWithKings.com /resources.

4. **Pray.** Fall on your face somewhere private and don't get up until your heart breaks. Leverage points 1 and 2 in this list and let the God of creativity and compassion break your heart into an outpouring of love in action.

As Nehemiah prayed and fasted, his feelings and convictions intensified.

First find your *why*. Then find your *way*.

Lesson: People with the strongest convictions have the greatest impacts. And conviction can be cultivated.

Action: Get clear on your *why*.

WHAT

This is what I'm considering or have begun:

WHY

This is why it's worth my full commitment:

WAY

This is my next step:

8

ALL IN

"All progress takes place outside the comfort zone." —Michael John Bobak

"I confess the sins we Israelites, including myself and my father's family, have committed against you." —Nehemiah 1:6

Instead of reaching down to pull up, step down and walk together.

Regardless if Nehemiah was guilty of every sin—regardless if he was as "bad" as others—he identified with the group confession. He claimed the sins of the whole as his own. *We're all the same. We're all in need. God help us!*

St. Augustine wrote, "The confession of evil works is the first beginning of good works."

Don't miss this. Nehemiah did not compare, contrast, or split hairs. He entered a guilty plea, throwing himself in with the condemned. It's not *their* problem. It's *our* problem.

Anne Lamott said that the most powerful sermon in the world is two words: "Me too."

In other words, you're communicating to your family, friends, and neighbors in need: *I can relate. You're not alone. I'm in this with you.*

If you've ever been alone and exposed, you know how uplifting it feels when someone comes to your defense and has your back. *If I know they're with me, I can make it through this.*

Yet truly identifying with someone will cost you. Commitment is not cheap. There's a reason heroes are hard to come by. When so many are building their brands and protecting their platforms, it's difficult to find men and women sacrificially committed to the welfare of others.

We've said that the only truly great endeavors are those that seek to serve. But just *seeking* to serve is not enough. Anyone can have a sympathetic thought and want good for another. To *do something* is what we're after.

Go all in

1. by empathizing and aligning with those you seek to serve, and
2. by committing yourself to the cause.

It's not until you fully commit that you etch your name in the foundation of a preferred future.

POTENTIAL

When I agreed to lead our church, the "me too" commitment had been made. I believed I was the same—just like anyone else—not better, not worse, but co-struggling through this beautiful mess called life, desperate for my daily drip of mercy and grace. But I was holding back some chips, and I sensed that God was asking me to go "all in."

Up until three years ago, I was a 90 percenter. I had grown up with natural talent, enough charisma to get by, and I was smart enough to stay ahead. But as the eldest, an example, and a role model, I felt the heavy burden of having it all together.

The harness of expectation saved me from many mistakes, but it also held me hostage. I was not free—free to dance, free to experiment, free to run, free to be me—the good, bad, and ugly. Instead, I hedged my bets. Failure didn't seem a reasonable option, so I was unlikely to attempt anything that presented a high risk of loss or embarrassment.

When I took a stab at something, I invested at 90 percent. That way, if I lost, I knew it wasn't failure. I wasn't totally invested. I didn't *really* try. It wouldn't define me because there was still more in me.

"You have so much potential," people told me. Nice.

I hated it.

Potential is this nebulous future version of myself that looks back at me from "someday" and points and laughs at the slacker I am today. There's no step-by-step manual for unlocking my personal potential. It's just a sticker on my forehead reminding me that I'm not there yet.

Bitter life circumstances led me to a counselor's office one afternoon with my wife, Hilary. Hilary talked through tears about feeling I wasn't present or happy or satisfied with her. My heart was both sad and detached. About thirty minutes into the dialogue, the counselor had me pegged. She went to her closet and pulled out a rope. (Tools of the trade, I guess.) She handed one end to me and kept the other firmly in her grasp. She started moving away, toward the opposite side of the room.

"I'm your 'potential,'" she said. And she pulled the rope.

She pulled harder, like she wanted me to fall out of my seat.

"Should I stand up?" I asked, so as not to disappoint. She yanked the rope, and I took it as a yes and stood up.

"I'm your 'potential,'" she said, this time almost mockingly. She pulled me farther. I was following her toward the other side of the room.

"Now, look back at your wife," she instructed. I did. Hilary was crying and about eight feet away. But the space between us seemed much farther.

"How do you feel, Hilary?" the counselor asked.

"Alone."

"Is that how you feel in your marriage?"

"Yes."

Crap.

But I got it. It clicked.

My so-called "potential" was robbing me of the present moment. Like an after-school bully, my potential was pulling me out of the here-and-now and taunting me with some preferred future that didn't exist.

What exists is *right now*. Now is what's real. The future is shaped by making the most of the present.

Ignore the future's shadow.

Reject the fear of failure.

Embrace this moment.

Oh, the places you'll go … if you can first embrace the place you are.

If you can embrace where you are and who you are, you can be free and empowered, and you can have the faith to go all in for what's next. You can risk; you can leap with both feet into the next right decision.

Nehemiah didn't justify himself. He didn't protect himself or hold back in case things didn't go well. Instead, he threw himself at the feet of the God of the universe, lumping himself in with the actions of a rebellious, stubborn people. It didn't matter that most of their guilt stemmed from actions before Nehemiah was even born. The fact that he was here (in the palace) and they were there (in Jerusalem) was irrelevant. And, as we'll soon see, Nehemiah blows through any fears or insecurities about his "potential," abandoning upward mobility in the kingdom of Persia for the sake of his desperate people.

Here's a simplified version of Nehemiah's prayer:

God, I'm like them.
We've all gone wrong.
We need you.
I'll be all in if you'll be with me.

BURN THE SHIPS

In 1519, Captain Hernán Cortés and his crew landed in Veracruz to begin his great conquest. Legend has it that Cortés instructed his men to burn the ships behind them.

Cortés: "We're here. Now burn the ships."

Rational subordinate: "You mean the ships we sailed here on?"

Cortés: "Exactly."

Rational subordinate: "Ha, ha. You so crazy, Cortés!"

Cortés: "I'm not joking."

Rational subordinate: "Well, then, you're a nutcase!"

Cortez: "Perhaps. Now burn the ships! Every. Last. One."

Retreat is easy when it's an option.

When you burn the option, there's no discussion of turning back. And there's no tolerance for 90 percent. All in and complete commitment are the name of the game.

Three years ago, I had wanted to be an author, a keynote speaker, and a spiritual entrepreneur (if that's a thing). But of this I am sure: *Today, I'm a pastor, in Orange County, California … to the people of this great community. And my family and I are all in for the sake of the people here.*

For me, "all in" means that the people of Orange County and I are in this together. We're all the same. And my family and I are here, in the trenches, in need of God to show up and do what only God can do—change lives.

All in means that Hilary and I uprooted and moved into the geographical center of the action. And we've never regretted it; we've never looked back.

All in means that I put my outside speaking and writing on hold to invest 100 percent in the church and build new momentum.

We've had to reaffirm our commitment to be all in every time we launched an additional service or took a big risk with no guarantee of success. Each bold step requires a re-up on faith and alignment. *We're doing this. We're giving it everything we've got. We're burning the ships.*

Yoda famously said, "Try not. Do, or do not. There is no try."

If you try, you're not committed. You've left all kinds of wiggle room and space for half measures. But if you commit to *do*, you're all in. And when you're all in, you find a way. Failure is possible—but not feared. Failure to the committed is simply a building block toward future success.

Don't *try*. Do. And go all in.

No hedging bets. No dancing around commitment. No guarding against embarrassment. You're in. You're in with *them* ... you're committed ... and you'll find a way.

Remember Nehemiah, and let his example inspire you. He didn't hedge his bets. He didn't have a parachute or an escape hatch.

"I'm with them, God. Me too. Have mercy on us. I'm willing to give up everything for the burden you've put in my heart. No more screwing around. Let's do this." And you're about to see that Nehemiah backs up his prayer with radical action. He's about to do something crazy.

Lesson: Less than 100 percent commitment is not commitment.

Action: Identify which ships need to burn, and specify what difficult decisions you're going to need to make in order to go all in. Then tell a trusted friend about your commitment.

Someone once said, "I don't understand your specific brand of crazy, but I do admire your total commitment to it." And that reminds me of this verse: "If we are 'out of our mind,' as some say, it is for God; if we are in our right mind, it is for you."[19]

9

FAVOR WITH KINGS

"Each person holds so much power within themselves that needs to be let out. Sometimes they just need a little nudge, a little direction, a little support, a little coaching, and the greatest things can happen." —Pete Carroll, coach

"Give your servant success today by granting him favor in the presence of this man." —Nehemiah 1:11

Every great project begins with a blessing.[20]

Someone says, "Yes, do it." An investor writes a check. A parent coaches with love. An employer gives the green light. A mentor urges, "You can do this." A spouse says, "I believe in you."

Nehemiah had something straight in his mind that many of us get confused. It's one of the mystical but important secrets of the universe. Some chalk this concept up to fortune, karma, or dumb luck, but it's more than that.

Favor comes from God, but it comes through kings. Of course it doesn't come exclusively from kings, but it does come from people in places of authority or significance in our lives. It's God who gives favor—blessing, opportunity, approval—but he gives it through people in positions of authority.

Yes, I'm talking about raises, promotions, bonuses, and new opportunities. I'm also talking about investors, politicians, government agencies, governing boards, and customers. And I include spouses, whose lack of support could make the effort futile. Regardless if you like it, you are forever influenced and acted upon by other people. You are never fully and finally independent or autonomous. Short of moving to an undiscovered island and living off the grid and off the land (and being devastatingly lonely), other humans will have something to do with your reaching and accomplishing your dreams.

God gives favor, blessing, and opportunity, and he gives them through *people*.

For Nehemiah, it was King Artaxerxes, the Persian ruler. Nehemiah wasn't born a king. He was born a Hebrew kid in the Persian Empire, eight hundred miles from his homeland. Artaxerxes was born a prince and then became king after his father was murdered.

Was Artaxerxes smarter than everyone else? Not likely. Was he more strategic or charismatic or a better visionary? Maybe. Probably not. But he was king. And Nehemiah's opinion of this Persian ruler didn't matter. Artaxerxes was king, and Nehemiah was not. So Nehemiah respected his king and employer. He honored him, served him, and as we'll see, earned Artaxerxes's friendship and respect.

Someone is in a position of authority over you—a boss, manager, trainer, CEO, captain, instructor, pastor, or board. It doesn't matter if they are ignorant, apathetic, or seem like they're out to get you. They are king. And you need them.

This is a theme throughout the Scriptures, notably referenced in the book of Daniel: "The Most High is sovereign over all kingdoms on earth and gives them to anyone he wishes."[21]

God puts leaders in authority—or at least allows them to have authority—for seasons of time. And God has designed the universe so that authority and structure matter.

The same week I was asked to take over the leadership of Mariners Church in Huntington Beach, I began praying this prayer: "God, give me favor with the leaders of Mariners, the city officials in Huntington Beach, and the people who will come to this church."

Over the past three years, an unexplainable yet undeniable generosity has been expressed toward my family and me by all three parties I just mentioned. We've received assistance to purchase a home that would have otherwise been impossible for us in this town. Our church has seen city-zoning designations shift so that we could acquire a new property. And the church itself is vibrant and flourishing, having grown 500 percent in that time frame.

I could try to take credit for it, but I know better. Some would say that I simply found the right place at the right time. And I would say … *exactly*!

Right place. Right time. Right staff. Right mentor. Right family. Right, *because of God's favor and blessing*. And God's blessings pass through people. His favor flows from one to another.

Consider another scenario. Nehemiah could have sensed from God that this was the project—the vision worth giving his life to—then cultivated conviction until he had the courage to leave the palace, and then … left. He could have packed his bags and sneaked off to Jerusalem under the cover of night, abandoning his post as cupbearer to avoid conflict. I'm sure he considered it. I imagine it seemed safer than what he was about to ask the king. But he didn't sneak off. He knew that the vision and the project would have a stronger chance of success if the king blessed it.

Nehemiah prayed for God to give him favor with the king.

Who is your "king"?

If you're between eighteen and thirty, you might be particularly prone to being impatient with those above you in the organizational structure. You might, in fact, hate organizational structures. But look at every successful entrepreneur or visionary. They all have structures. The more successful you are, the bigger your structure becomes. Then you find that you are at the head of the very thing you resented when you were younger.

Organizations are not the enemy. The enemy is the enemy. Don't get caught up in personal and petty battles. Your fight is much bigger.[22] And you need favor to make the most of your opportunities.

WIN FRIENDS AND INFLUENCE KINGS

You need people. They might make you crazy, but you probably make them just as crazy. You can have strong convictions and high expectations while still keeping a soft heart.

Here are a few insights to consider as you pray for favor while seeking to honor those around and above you:

You can learn something from everyone. You have never met a person from whom you cannot learn. Don't waste time bent over the issues of conflict. Find the points of connection and learn. Uncover the genius of your superiors by asking questions. I never show up to a meeting with my boss without a question I can pose. I will brainstorm questions as I drive to the meeting. He's been leading a church for thirty years. I've been leading a church for three. If I think I have nothing left to learn from him, I'm delusional.

Act on advice. There are few things more annoying than people who ask for my time, listen to my advice, and then ignore what I tell them. Why would I continue to make time for people who don't listen or don't have the courage to follow through? However, those who listen, act, and pass on wisdom are people I'll support in achieving their dreams.

Embrace the core and contextualize the rest. If leaders are going to support your project, vision, or idea, they'll want to know that you align with the principles with which they feel most strongly. If you're starting a new project but you want the support and resources of the original, larger organization or entity to help you get off the ground, then you had better know what the non-negotiables are and sign on the line. The peripheral gets blurry and should have freedom to be shaped by unique goals, chemistry, and context, but the core is the core. The main things are the main things. DNA is DNA. And if you want the support of the powers that be, honor what they view to be the main thing. If you honor the core, you honor your leaders. Another way of saying it is this: *build on shoulders; don't stomp on toes.*

Innovate, don't irritate. Creative and innovative people can go terribly wrong when they allow their attitudes to shift from helpful innovation to hostile irritation. We get it; the system is broken. Don't complain. Fix it. If you're someone who identifies needs *and* solves problems, you'll never lack work—or support.

Pray. Even if you don't think you're the praying type, God is the ultimate authority and he's *for you*. He gives you the desires that fuel and fill your heart.[23] He's always been there, and he's here now, with you, guiding you, whispering to you, prompting action, and giving you clarity and courage for the next right step. Take it. And pray for favor.

I know it makes you feel vulnerable. I know you'd prefer not to *need* anyone's approval and just to follow your heart and your instincts instead. I get it. But you and I need to keep the following in mind:

Favor means blessing.

Favor means resources.

Favor means belief and backing.

Favor means wisdom and guidance.

Favor means you're not alone. God is with you, divinely orchestrating the influencers in your life.

Consider that God's favor might not come from the first person who pops into your mind—the default boss or authority figure in your life. It might. Or it might come through someone else. Authority figures get a choice too. They can choose to participate in the work or not. You can't control others. But you can use self-control and wait for God to extend his favor on your vision somehow, some way.

Don't leave home without it.

Lesson: God gives favor—but he gives it through authorities.

Action: Identify your potential kings.

> Who are the authority figures in your life?
>
> Where have you run into dead ends?
>
> Where do you see what could be God's favor?
>
> What might honoring authority look like today?

Consider the following words from the apostle Paul to followers of Jesus in Rome:

> Everyone must submit to governing authorities. For all authority comes from God, and those in positions of authority have been placed there by God. So anyone who rebels against authority is rebelling against what God has instituted, and they will be punished. For the authorities do not strike fear in people who are doing right, but in those who are doing wrong. Would you like to live without fear of the authorities? Do what is right, and they will honor you. The authorities are God's servants, sent for your good. (Romans 13:1–4)

Certainly, there are exceptions to every rule, and there are times when disobeying a blatantly immoral or egregious demand is necessary. But as a general rule, honor authority.

10

EXCELLENCE

"Be a yardstick of quality. Some people aren't used to an environment where excellence is expected." —Steve Jobs

"I had not been sad in his presence before, so the king asked ..." —Nehemiah 2:1–2

Nehemiah's track record working for the king reminds me of a bumper sticker I saw: *"No bad days."*

Judging by the details in the story of Nehemiah, it seems Nehemiah worked faithfully for the Persian king without ever looking sad or out of sorts. It's safe to assume that Nehemiah had worked for the king for a number of years. The second chapter of Nehemiah makes it clear that the king respected Nehemiah, and the respect of people in high positions of leadership takes a long time to earn. Celebrities and senior leaders have small circles of trust, and few break in. Nehemiah had been a faithful servant who worked with excellence—every day. And the king noticed.

A friend of mine, Michael, owns a security company. He started his own business to get out from under the Hollywood bodyguard scene that had enmeshed him. Michael had been a personal bodyguard for several high-profile families. His position made him physically close to sports and entertainment elites, but it was his demeanor, character, and commitment to excellence that put him in the inner circle.

It took several years, but two famous families welcomed Michael into their lives. He became much more than a bodyguard. He drove the kids to school, got groceries, cooked meals, traveled on family vacations, and at times would sit, relax, eat, drink, and watch TV with the family. He became a trusted friend.

I believe that's what happened in Nehemiah's case. He became a trusted friend. He earned favor through faithfulness to his employer.

God gives favor through other people, and the way you become an easy target for favor is by working with excellence. Today. Not later, when you like your job more or hang out with celebrities. Today.

Are you a stay-at-home parent? Teacher? Personal trainer? Salesperson? Manager? Executive assistant? Marketing guru? Nonprofit leader? Whatever your position, find something meaningful about today's work, then work with excellence and give your best. Men and women who give their best today receive better opportunities tomorrow.

Even if you want to get out of your company, job, or industry, opportunity has a way of finding those who have made the most of past opportunities. Don't waste today.

YOUR BEST

I recently read an article about Matt Williams, a Major League Baseball coach and former player. Past and present teammates commented on Williams's intensity, completive nature, and how he enjoyed showing up to work every day. The writer summarized Williams's reputation for hard work and preparedness by saying, "He picked up the reputation as a player-friendly coach who prepared for every contest as if it were Game 7 of the World Series."[24]

That reminded me of a lesson I learned as a child from my dad: "Show up every day and give it your best. When you're doing your best, you don't have to worry about wins and losses. They have a way of taking care of themselves."

My friend Taylor's dad told him, "Son, while you're playing video games, your opponent is working on his jump shot."

More recently, my pastor-mentor Kenton Beshore coached me, saying, "Prepare and bring your best every Sunday. Prepare the same way to speak to one hundred people as you would before speaking to ten thousand people. If you don't, you'll never speak to ten thousand people."

How hard do you work? Are you bringing your best?

Excellence now leads to opportunity later.

It was true in Nehemiah's story. It worked for Michael. And it's worked for millions of people throughout history who have accomplished great things.

Here are habits that people who work day after day with excellence put into practice:

Show up early and ready. Being on time shows commitment and that you honor other people's time. Being prepared shows that you care, are capable, and have a vision for making the most of the opportunity. People in charge love to see commitment, almost more than anything else.

Bring energy and enthusiasm. There are people in my life who give me energy, and there are people who drain my energy. I try to maximize my time with the former and minimize my time with the latter. Don't be a drain. Find ways to motivate yourself. Keep energized and enthusiastic about the work at hand. Some days, that's easy. Other days, it's not. The key is to keep a good attitude, regardless of circumstances. You do that by focusing on the bigger picture and a bigger God.

Spend time with people who work with excellence. You become like the people who surround you. The more time you spend with someone, the greater the influence they have on your life. That might be depressing—you can't pick your family or the person in the next cubicle—but there's a bright side. You can choose to be influenced in all kinds of ways: books, movies, church, conferences, music, podcasts. Also, be intentional about your friends. Your friendships don't all need to be strategic—you have to *like* your friends—but your friendships should be deliberate, and they should encourage you to be more of the person you desire to be.

Develop healthy rhythms. By definition, the healthy flourish. You can't be excellent and sick. When you're sick, your body deploys all available resources to fight off the threat to your physical health. That's what makes you lethargic and want to lie down. Investigate what it means to manage your energy. Build healthy habits in all areas of your life—physically, mentally, emotionally, spiritually.

Block time for the main things. Stephen Covey said, "The main thing is to keep the main thing the main thing." He means that most things don't matter. So don't get distracted by lesser things. Prioritize what matters most and build appropriate windows of time into your calendar to accomplish the things that really matter.

Never stop learning. Don't get complacent and lazy. There's always more to learn. Without becoming obsessed and making those closest to you miserable, dedicate yourself to healthy progress ... and keep learning. Have a book you're reading in every room of your house. Listen to podcasts instead of the radio in the car. Schedule time for personal growth—put it in the calendar like an appointment you can't break.

Commit to excellence. Not perfection. But progress that points you in the direction of excellence.

Lesson: Working with excellence now paves the way to future opportunity.

Action: Rank the habits listed in this chapter in order of easiest to most difficult for you. Focus on one of the habits this week. Visit one or both of the pages below for additional resources to go further faster on this and related topics:

FavorWithKings.com

CalebAnderson.tv

11

PRAY + PLAN

"Pray as though everything depended on God. Work as though everything depended on you." —St. Augustine

*"The king said to me, 'What is it you want?' Then …
I answered the king …"* —Nehemiah 2:4–5

My wife, Hilary, is from the Seattle area. I've already mentioned that she and I lived there a few years after we were married. The gloomy gray and constant drizzle got to me. But there was a silver lining. I'm a University of Southern California alum, and during my senior year, a coach named Pete Carroll came to USC and sparked an incredible turnaround. Unfortunately, he didn't come to coach my volleyball team; he coached football. Still, I became a big Pete Carroll fan. So, naturally, when I was living in Seattle and Pete put on the green and blue of the Seahawks, I became a fan of the team.

One of the Seahawks' slogans is this: "*The separation is in the preparation.*"

The difference between a normal NFL team and a great NFL team is slight. Little commitments to preparation when no one is looking are what set apart Super Bowl winners.

Nehemiah might have had some Pete Carroll in him. When the moment of truth arrived for Nehemiah, he was ready. He was prepared.

Nehemiah had grieved the bad news, cultivated conviction, chosen to go all in, prayed for favor, and then (in chapter 2, verses 1–4) the king of all the land asks him what's bothering him and what he wants to do about it.

Favor in progress.

The king cares about Nehemiah and is willing to help. Blank-check time!

But this is a pivotal moment. Things could still go downhill from here.

What if Nehemiah said, "I don't know"? Or what if he stuttered, paused, looked at his feet, and said, "Uh … I didn't expect you to care, so I'm not prepared."

Disaster. Respect would have been lost, the opportunity forfeited, and the issue would've been off the king's radar. If Nehemiah didn't care enough to be prepared, the king certainly would not have cared.

If *you* don't care enough to be prepared, no one else will care enough to support you.

In great stories, heroes are prepared.

Nehemiah had faith in the God who gives favor through kings.

Nehemiah feared the King of the universe more than the king of Persia. And he expected a miracle of favor and prepared for his moment of truth.

"What is it you want?"

SIGHT

Some four hundred years after Nehemiah's moment of truth, another man had his own moment of truth. He's referred to as a blind beggar named Bartimaeus, sitting harmlessly outside a famous city called Jericho.[25] When blind Bartimaeus heard an unusual ruckus and the shuffling of a mob of people, he started asking passersby, "Guys … hey … what's going on here?"

"Jesus of Nazareth is coming this way," someone told him.

Something leaped in the blind man's soul. Hope was rising, and with no filter or social awareness, he began shouting at the top of his lungs, "Jesus … have mercy on me!"

Jesus was mysterious. His touch felt like home and his words pierced with heaven's power. People called him teacher, but it was understood that he was much more than that. His popularity was growing by the day, and he was the first topic of conversation at water coolers and pubs.

Naturally, there were people with agendas wanting to be close to Jesus and make themselves seem significant by association. Several men acted as though they were leading this crowd and protecting Jesus from the masses. When they heard the blind man recklessly shouting from the curb, they glared at him and used know-your-place words to try to shut him up. It didn't work.

Our bold blind guy shouted even louder, "Savior, have mercy on me!"

The desperate, blind beggar was committed. He had faith that Jesus was different. Jesus could do more for him than drop some coins in his cup.

When Jesus heard the persistent faith of the blind beggar, he stopped. The crowd also stopped, trying to avoid a game of human dominoes. Jesus ordered the men who were trying to look important to go and get the blind man they had rejected from the curb and bring him to Jesus.

Jesus asked Bartimaeus, "What do you want me to do for you?"

Moment of truth.

Nehemiah's moment of truth was face to face with the king of Persia. Bartimaeus's moment of truth was face to face with the King of the universe in the flesh.

Maybe there was an upside to being blind. If I had looked into the eyes of Jesus—creator of heaven and earth—standing there in human skin, I probably would have peed myself.

But our faithful, undeterred man with diseased eyes responded with humble clarity and confidence.

"Lord, I want to see."

"Receive your sight; your faith has healed you," Jesus replied.

And the blind man could see.

PARTNERING IN MIRACLES

What will your faith do for you? Are you prepared for your miracle? What if God were passing by? Do you know what you'd ask of him?

We pray ... and we plan.

We're dependent on God ... and we're working with excellence.

We're listening ... and we're executing a dream.

It's both. It's a divine-human partnership. There's a mystery to it. There's a part that only God can play—miracles that only God can do. And there's preparation and work in which you and I daily engage.

"In their hearts humans plan their course, but the Lord establishes their steps."[26]

Ultimately, God is running the show. But you'll be more apt to play your role if you're praying and preparing ... and paying attention. Jesus might be walking by.

PRAYER-BOARDING

Have you heard of dream-boarding? It's the practice of putting on paper—or poster board—images, words, and pictures that express your dreams and goals for the coming year. The exercise has several benefits:

1. **Intentional planning.** You have to spell out what it is you want to see and find images that represent that goal. Articulating your intention is movement toward action.

2. **Visualization.** Moving from thought or theory to a more literal image is an important step. Say, for example, that you want to raise money to build a playground at a lower-income community park this

year. Instead of just thinking that thought in your head, cut out a picture of an awesome playground with kids on it and glue it on a poster board. The visual helps it become more real in your mind.

3. **Focus.** Keeping the visual in front of you—posted in your closet or office—reaffirms your intention and refocuses your engagement each day. We humans have a propensity to forget and need regular reminders of our commitments.

Let's take this dream-board concept and steer it a bit more toward Nehemiah's example. The principles are solid; we need only add the prayer component.

I know that Nehemiah didn't have a Staples store in Persia where he could pick up poster board, but I still believe that he mapped out his plan. He defined it. Visualized it. Reaffirmed and refocused on it. He sketched out in dirt or on a stone what it might look like to rebuild the wall of Jerusalem. Then he prayed, knowing that even with his best intentions, this would be a divine-human partnership.

Plan. Pray. Prayer-board.

GOD OF DETAILS

We saw in chapter 1 of Nehemiah's memoirs that he prayed and fasted and listened for God. In chapter 2, we see that Nehemiah also made very deliberate plans, expecting God to give him favor with the king of Persia.

King: "You've never looked sad like this. What's wrong?"

Nehemiah: "My homeland has been burned and is still in ruins. My family and friends live in vulnerability and disgrace."

King: "What is it that you want?"

With a prayer to the God of heaven, I replied ...[27]

The Bible says that in that moment, Nehemiah prayed to the God of heaven—in his spirit—before answering the king. Nehemiah remembered where favor comes from. Favor comes *through* kings, but it comes *from* the King of Kings.

Then he responds to King Artaxerxes ...

Nehemiah: "Please allow me to go to my ancestors' city and rebuild."

King: "How long will it take, and what do you need?"

Nehemiah replied confidently and set a time frame.

The text also indicates that the queen was sitting with the king. I wonder if that was part of Nehemiah's strategy and planning. He probably mentions that fact in his detailed journal because the queen influenced the king in this decision. Had he been alone, the king might have been less compassionate. I believe that Nehemiah planned and prayed for an occasion when the queen would be at the king's side.

Nehemiah: "Also, King and Queen, I'd like to make a few more requests. I've thought this whole project through, and it will require

1. letters to local governors along the journey for safety,
2. a letter to the lumberyard indicating this is a government-sponsored project, and
3. army officers and troops for protection."

And he got it. All of it.

Favor.

Nehemiah's prayer and planning paid off in a miracle from God.

In great stories, heroes are prepared and partner with God in miracles.

You are living a great story.

Lesson: Pray for favor and miracles from God; plan and be prepared for opportunities to present themselves.

Action: Make a prayer-board. Think through as much of the project as you can. Picture outcomes. Plan for what you'll need. Consider planning in stages. Nehemiah loaded up with lumber and metal supplies knowing that he'd need them down the road.

Ask yourself: What will I need in …

Phase 1?

Phase 2?

Phase 3?

Pray that God would bring the resources. Write down your prayers, and keep praying them. Put visuals (prayer-board) in front of you to keep the vision fresh in your mind.

12

WHEN THINGS
GET REAL

*"If you are not willing to risk the usual, you will
have to settle for the ordinary."* —*Jim Rohn*

*"They were very much disturbed that someone had come to
promote the welfare of the Israelites."* —*Nehemiah 2:10*

The above verse from Nehemiah is the first indication of adversity.
There is no story without adversity. And the greater the story, the
more challenging the opposition.

Nehemiah would come up against a dark principle of this broken world: There are people in power who don't want others to have
power. There are forces of evil that operate through people preserving
self-interest at the expense of others. We'll talk more about opposition

later, but for now, it's important to know this: after finding favor and
the blessing to move forward, there is a reality check.

After all, there is no easy way of traveling eight hundred miles,
sleeping on the side of the road, patrolling while you rest to ensure
protection of your investment, eating what you kill, and trying to
keep your support system positive just to get to the starting point
where the hard work begins.

Then, of course, as you enter the territory where your dream will
become work, you are greeted with an antagonistic what-do-you-
think-you're-doing-here welcome. Things got real. They always do.

If the path to accomplishing great things were easy, everyone
would be doing it. But it isn't.

STEP IN

Three hundred years before Nehemiah traveled from the palace of
Persia to the ruins of Jerusalem, a leader named Joshua faced his own
things-just-got-real moment. Following the death of Moses, Joshua
took over the responsibility of leading the people of Israel from the
desert and into what's known as the Promised Land.

Moses had become iconic. Joshua was relatively unknown. God
had been with Moses. Whether God was with Joshua was yet to be
determined.

And then, on a morning that felt different from any recent
morning, God asked Joshua to lead a million-plus people of Israel
across the Jordan River. But there was no bridge. And it was flood
season, so the waters were high and moving fast.

Things were about to get real.

"Have the priests carrying the ark of the covenant step into the water first," God instructed Joshua. "Then I'll make a way for the people to walk across."[28]

I imagine Joshua's inner dialogue went something like this:

"Sure, God. No problem. I'll just ask my most important leaders, who are also the most dignified and most opinionated, to carry the most valuable asset we have—the ark representing *your presence*—into the rushing water. Everyone will love this idea. And I'm a brand-new authority figure here, so what could possibly go wrong?

"By the way, God," Joshua's internal struggle continued, "Moses only had to lift up his staff from a comfortable, dry distance, and you parted the Red Sea. That seems like favoritism. You're not exactly making this easy on me."

God's instruction, reiterated: "Step in."

God is predictable in that he is always good. But he's unpredictable in how he expresses his goodness. This miracle would be *similar* to the first, not the same. This time, God wanted the people to get wet before he made the ground dry.

Picture the scene. Grown men carrying the famous ark of the covenant, which represented God's presence with his people. And they walked *into* a river during flood season. Before the guys carrying the back side of the ark step into the water, the poor guys in front are already chest deep! (I've been in the Jordan River and took one too many steps.)

Chest deep. Then comes the miracle. God parts the waters and the whole party dances their way to the land of Promise.

But first: chest deep.

Mariners Church Huntington Beach has been running four services at a public facility, setting up at 6:00 a.m. and tearing down at 8:00 p.m., week after week, for multiple years now. It's a pace we can't keep up, and it's a lease that will soon expire.

A year ago, knowing a change of venue would soon be necessary, we began raising money toward our future home—not yet knowing where it would be.

But the story of Joshua kept coming to my mind. "Step in ... and then I'll do the miracle."

In other words, *trust God for the miracle; do what you can do in the meantime to prepare and plan ahead. Step in now, at the risk of looking silly and getting wet.*

I remember standing up in front of all four services telling the church that we were going to raise money now believing that God would do a miracle later. Incredibly, the church responded with confidence.

And then, within two weeks, the city council of Huntington Beach voted to change a strict zoning ordinance so that religious gatherings—not just retail—were allowed to occupy one of the busiest intersections in Orange County.

About that same time, an old discount movie theater at the above-mentioned intersection, one that had turned down two of our requests to speak with them about our church using their property, suddenly reached out to us with a new willingness to make a deal.

"Step in ... and I'll do the miracle."

Still, there was a considerable amount of money to be raised. And how could I ask anyone else to give sacrificially to the renovation project unless my wife and I were sacrificing at a faith-producing level ourselves?

So Hilary and I did the hard work of looking over our budget, cutting whatever excess we could (e.g., cable TV, pedicures, meals out, and other creative cuts). We looked at what we thought we could save. Then we doubled the dollar amount. The total ended up being the equivalent of what we were already giving to the church on a normal month-to-month basis. For us, that felt like an intimidating sum of money. And we didn't know how we were going to do it. But we committed.

About that same time, I was submitting proposals for a book that lived in my head called *Favor with Kings*. It would be a couple of months before hearing back from any publishers. But when I did, I was amazed. Three major publishers wanted to pay me to write this book, including the publisher I chose, David C Cook. The advance for the book that's in your hands is allowing Hilary and me to fulfill our commitment to what our church called the Step In Campaign.

We named our effort to acquire and renovate the movie theater "Step In" based on the story of Joshua leading the Israelites into the water and then on to the Promised Land on dry ground.

You might not have a water problem, but there is something between you and the future that God has whispered to your heart. To get there, you're going to have to get wet. You might have to get chest deep before you see the next miracle.

Progress will cost you something—comfort at a minimum. But opposition, sacrifice, and steps of faith are part of the miraculous journey. There's no way around the river. You must go through it.

Good news: God is with you. Don't be afraid to get wet.

Lesson: At some point, God will ask you to step in—chest deep—before you see the miracle.

Action: Examine your budget this week. Where can you save? What can you cut? To take bold steps of faith, it helps to have more financial flexibility. Start now. Start small.

13

A FEW

"You can do what I cannot do. I can do what you cannot do. Together, we can do great things." —Mother Teresa

"I set out during the night with a few others." —Nehemiah 2:12

We don't know from Nehemiah's memoirs if the "few others" mentioned in chapter 2, verse 12, became an inner circle for Nehemiah. But we know that several people were selected for a reason (Nehemiah was intentional and strategic) and went with him during the night to examine the actual condition of the wall. Later, Nehemiah would stand with the masses. That night he surveyed with just a few.

"A few" is a recurring theme associated with people who accomplish great things—not only in the Bible, but anywhere you find significant achievements.

In recent decades, the great American companies have had iconic figureheads that embody their company legacies, but they were not stories of isolated success. Gates had Allen (Microsoft), Jobs had Wozniak and Wayne (Apple), Zuckerberg had Saverin, McCollum, Moskovitz, and Hughes (Facebook).

Billy Graham had his face on the posters, but it was his wife, Ruth, and Wilson, Barrows, and Shea who vaulted his influence.

Abraham Lincoln surrounded himself with a few trusted advisers, each having differing political perspectives.[29]

Martin Luther King Jr. traveled with a small, trusted entourage.

Mother Teresa became a famous nun, but she did not work alone. She worked alongside "a few" other nuns who shared a common mission: serve *the least of these*.[30]

In the prime of King David's leadership, when he was a conquering king, he kept a few *mighty men* at his side.[31]

Jesus had an inner circle of twelve disciples, and three of those were particularly trusted with extra access to Jesus. I believe that Jesus was God in skin. If *he* needed an inner circle of friends, who of us can survive without one?

You need a few good men or women in your life. No exceptions.

SUPPORT SYSTEM

I officiate fewer weddings than I used to, but I still frequently use these famous verses to affirm how important marriage, partnership, and togetherness are: "Two are better than one, because they have a good return for their labor: If either of them falls down, one can help the other up."[32]

Couples like these verses because they reinforce what they have personally experienced—life is better together. Together, we complement each other, make up for weaknesses, troubleshoot complex issues, test our theories, and perhaps most importantly, we pick each other up.

There are days when darkness seems as though it has the advantage—when you're down on the scoreboard and time is running out, when you're sick, tired, and out of options. It's at times like these when we need a nudge, a reminder, a voice that stands out from the condemning choir of boos. We need *a few*.

My two longest-lasting friends don't live in my same state, so communication is less frequent, but I've also sought out a local few—some who share my passion and support my projects. Like an informal board of directors, they meet with me periodically to process problems, evaluate opportunities, and encourage me to keep on. I'm modeling this evolving support system based on other groups I've seen be effective.

One mentor has what he calls his "Group of Six." He and five other men have met together regularly for thirty years. They have processed major business deals, leadership decisions, entrepreneurial launches, health issues, marriage and parenting struggles, and much more. They are advisers to one another, but not in the official "board" capacity. Friendship and spiritual conviction are their bond. Each credits the group with personal growth, spiritual guidance, wisdom, and encouragement.

Another friend and mentor has three men whom he calls whenever he travels. He's done so for the past twenty years, dating back to his NFL days. It's difficult to be the person you want to be when you're on the road—whether playing football, speaking to crowds, or consulting with executives—so having a support system in place is this guy's saving grace. He credits them with helping his marriage and his morale and for keeping him focused on what matters most.

Who are your "few"? It's okay if you don't have them yet. But it's not okay if you're not looking and praying for them. You're going to need a support system to do whatever it is you want to do. Start developing your few now by considering the following qualities you want in these friends.

Loyalty. Consistency matters. Your few will walk with you for years, not months. They should be able to see through the circumstances and support you when you're winning and when you're losing—when you're weak and when you're strong. Choose people who will have your back when the pressure mounts and demands weigh heavy. Some may have good intentions but be prone to distraction and have difficulty prioritizing anyone but themselves.

Experience. Invite a few people into your life who have lived longer, failed more, and persevered when it counted. Be suspicious of anyone who pretends not to have failed. Ideally, your few should have diverse experiences, backgrounds, and abilities.

Diligence. Your few don't necessarily need to have specific knowledge of your work or industry if they are great at asking questions and creating plans. Good advisers might slow you down, but only long enough to thoroughly evaluate the opportunity and approach. They will help you see things you can't see on your own. They will anticipate issues that might arise in various scenarios. Make sure you have someone in your life who is diligent and willing to ask enough questions to get below the surface of the issue at hand.

Levelheadedness. Your few can't be prone to hasty decision making or violating healthy process. If you're like me, you don't like "process." Process is slow. I like to move quickly. But having a trusted few with life experience and level heads will keep you and me from rushing into poor decisions or reacting too quickly to either good news or bad news.

Creativity. Everyone is creative, but not everyone applies creativity. You don't need an artist or designer on your team (though one would be nice) to have creativity. Creativity comes in all shapes and sizes. But it begins with observation. People who notice learn; people who learn explore; people who explore dream; and people who dream create, innovate, adapt, tweak, and repurpose for new applications or end arounds.

Monetary success is not the tell-all of a person's capacity to counsel, coach, or support you. Look for the listed characteristics in your *few*. And start looking now.

Resist what I call the "gig-friend" mind-set. I live close to Los Angeles and have a lot of friends in the city. Many of these friends have fallen victim to the temptation to hang out only with friends whom they're working with on a single project. This movie, these friends. Next movie, on to the next set of friends. New gig, new friends. And so the cycle of shallow relationships goes.

You should have some gig-friends. But you also want a *few* who will go the distance with you.

If you find it difficult to engage the kind of people you need for your future, ask yourself these painful questions: Am I such a person? Am I loyal? Do I have experiences others would value? Am I levelheaded, diligent, creative? Your relationships won't work if they are just about you—serving your needs. Begin by *being* a loyal friend to someone who has these kinds of people in his or her life already. Listen. Learn.

And then, do what Nehemiah did. Ask your friend to take a ride with you.

Lesson: We all need a few trusted advisers.

Action: Find your few. List all the people you know who have the qualities we listed in this chapter. Circle the ideal four you'd like to do life with. Reach out to them. Give them a copy of this book and talk about what it would look like to support one another over the long haul.

14

SEE AND LEARN

"It's not what you look at that matters, it's what you see." —Anonymous

"By night I went out through the Valley Gate ... examining the walls of Jerusalem, which had been broken down." —Nehemiah 2:13

How do you tell people that their house stinks? It's awkward, and you probably won't, unless you're forced to have to frequent the foul domicile.

The problem is that the people living in the odor cave don't smell it. It crept in on them like a sneaky villain or like heat on a frog in a boiling pot. Before they know anything is wrong, they are sick and have no friends.

You have to want to know your house stinks. Vigilant fresh making is required.

I say that to help you see this: the Israelites got desensitized to the funk.

NOTICE

One of Nehemiah's suspicions was confirmed upon arrival. The people living in Jerusalem could not see what needed to be done. They knew the walls were broken down, but seeing them that way every day had become desensitizing. After one or more early attempts at reconstruction, they gave up. They stopped seeing how bad things were, and they stopped believing life could be different. They had settled back in Jerusalem, and then they *settled* again into complacency, or a sense of normalcy.

The people of Jerusalem needed the catalytic voice of Nehemiah to move them from what was to what could be. But first, Nehemiah needed to see the reality for himself. Before any *Braveheart* speeches, prior to the rallying of the troops or putting plans in motion, Nehemiah went by night to assess the situation.

Assess what *is* to articulate what *could be*.

You have conviction and commitment, you're praying for favor, and you're making plans—all because there is something unique that God has put inside of you that needs to work its way out into tangible reality. Something has to be done that others have overlooked.

They don't see it. They're walking right past the opportunity every day. They've become so used to business as usual that they're settling and stuck. You, however, know something needs to change. But before you start telling the world, take *a few* and get up close and personal with the truth of the matter.

It's time to assess the current realities honestly. You have to know what's really going on if you're going to be used to spark meaningful change. Nehemiah took a few men, went out at night, and got a good, long look at the true state of affairs.

VALLEY GATE

Consider the last time you listened to someone talk about his or her story or life journey. What stood out to you? You might have been impressed by the mountaintop conquests and achievements, but it was likely the difficulty, disappointment, and struggle that you related to. It was the low points—the valleys of their losses, insecurities, and defeats—that caused you to connect emotionally to the person. Pain and struggle are common to the human experience, and they are the very things that bond perfect strangers.

I believe that's why Nehemiah mentioned that he went through the Valley Gate (as opposed to one of the other eleven gates). "Valley" in Scripture references the low points in life. Mountaintops are the highs; valleys are the lows. Nehemiah was suggesting that he went to the low point of Jerusalem to see the true, honest state of affairs. It's from this vantage point that the climb toward "better" can begin.

Nehemiah noted that he went through the Valley Gate because he wanted to communicate connection with the plight of the people. He wanted to show that he wasn't afraid of the valley his people found themselves in. He embraced it and would allow God to use it for good.

People on platforms often try to impress a crowd with their accomplishments, but it's being honest about your authentic struggles that encourages listeners. Humans respect success and accomplishment, but we connect to failure and pain.

As the shepherd-songwriter David sang,

> Even though I walk
> through the darkest valley,

I will fear no evil,

    for you are with me.[33]

God was with David.

God has always been with his people.

And as we'll continue to see, God was with Nehemiah—in the valley of struggle.

EMBRACE THE STRUGGLE

I've been with my brother, Aaron, and my sister-in-law, Amber, this week as I'm writing. Amber is a great young interior designer. She recently left another firm because she was humiliated and belittled by the hoity-toity owner. (Think *Devil Wears Prada*.) At first, the experience demoralized Amber and made her insecure. But she has since turned it around.

Amber told Hilary and me last night that what she learned from the painful experiences of her past employment is shaping how she wants to run her own business going forward. She will work with high standards of excellence, yet she will also look to serve. For instance, she's donating some of her time to help families who can't afford an interior designer but need help de-cluttering, upgrading, simplifying, and creating clean, welcoming environments.

"The interior design business has become one of arrogant wealth and status design. I want to change that and help people process what really matters to them, simplifying their homes and lives while upgrading the functionality of their space," she told me.[34]

Amber's personal valley has led to a conviction that helps her relate to, and thereby serve, more people. For her, business is not just about making money. It's about making a difference in people's lives.

Enter through the Valley Gate and connect with people in the middle of reality. It's struggle and difficulty that lead to the best breakthroughs and most meaningful achievements.

Don't be that person who is always making up stuff about what you're doing or what's about to go down. Live in the reality of what is—the good, the bad, and the ugly. You'll never get *up there* if you're not building on the honest foundation of *down here*.

NO ASSUMPTIONS

Imagine if Nehemiah had ridden into town, set up a stage, and started barking out ignorant orders. It wouldn't have worked. No one listens to the arrogant assumptions of someone who clearly hasn't done the work of studying the problem.

Nehemiah studied the problem before he offered any solutions.

If you're starting a business, talk to your customers. What do they want? What is their pain? What motivates them? Dig in, listen, connect.

If you're starting a new nonprofit or ministry, identify the real needs. Who are the people? What are their stories? What do they feel they need? What else do they need beyond what they can articulate today?

Whatever the opportunity you're moving toward, you need to discover what it is you *don't know*. You don't know what you don't know, but someone does. Ask veterans. Find mentors. Research. Don't make assumptions.

Go and see for yourself.

Enter through the Valley Gate of people's authentic struggles.

It's usually our pride or impatience that will cut short this learning process. Take the time. Listen to stories. Find guides. See and learn.

Lesson: Listen, learn, and connect with people's authentic struggles.

Action: Research the realities. Listen to stories. Find guides.
And don't miss this opportunity to honestly evaluate your own life. Pause here for a moment and ask yourself these questions:

What am I settling for in my life that I could change, build, fix, or make better?

What have I stopped seeing or become desensitized to?

Will I trust a *few* others to tell me the truth?

15

WORDS CREATE WORLDS

*"I know nothing in the world that has as much
power as a word." —Emily Dickinson*

"Then I said to them, 'You see …'" —Nehemiah 2:5

Eric became a friend, but he started as a man-crush. You'd understand if you met him. At six foot three and with 225 pounds of
pure muscle, this African American motivational speaker leverages
his background in the NFL, but he doesn't depend on it. His confident, caring presence speaks for itself. And his articulate passion and
humorous insights can win any crowd.

Eric introduced himself to me after I spoke at his home church.
"You've got a gift," he told me. I loved hearing that. One of the best
things in the world is having someone affirm that you're "gifted"

in some way and that you're using that gift in an effective manner. Especially when, in your own mind, you feel like you're underachieving and reaching your "potential" at a snail's pace.

"Thank you," I replied, probably looking down.

"Seriously. I speak for a living, and you have a rare ability to communicate and connect with an audience," Eric continued.

I'd never met the man, but he was determined to speak life into me—a perfect stranger. He could probably tell that I wanted to believe his words but that I was distracted by different, opposing words in my head.

"You speak for a living? I'd love to know more about that," I told him, shifting the focus off me.

"How long are you in town?" he asked me.

"I just moved here. I think it's temporary, but I'm sure I'll be here at least a year."

"Then I want you to come to a seminar I'm doing at the end of the month, no charge. I'd just love to have you as my guest."

The rest is history. Eric Boles immediately became a friend and mentor. I've learned a great deal from Eric, and he was someone who believed in me during a tough transition in my life.

One lesson I learned from Eric correlates to Nehemiah's story. I still remember sitting in an office chair around a rectangular table in a lecture room with forty people I didn't know. Most of them were on staff at a local hospital in the area—paying customers for Eric's presentation. Eric launched in, and I opened my workbook. The pen was in my hand and I was hungry for more encouragement.

"Your mind is on autopilot 95 percent of the time," he said. "Most of your life—almost all your decisions—are trained, predetermined, learned behaviors based on experiences and data from your past stored in your subconscious. And many of you are operating based off of old, unhelpful information."

He offered scientific research, personal examples, and exercises, but I knew his general point was true from the start. And I knew I had old data from past experiences in the operating system of my subconscious that was not helping me. In fact, I came to discover that I had limiting beliefs about myself and how the world works that were hurting me.

"Time to introduce new data," Eric declared.

Bring it.

AFFIRMATIONS

Sure, there are cheesy, sleazy examples of self-help gone wrong. But here's my stance: All truth is God's truth. So I don't care where it comes from. I don't care what it's labeled. If it's healthy, helpful, and true, then I'm for it.

If you think self-help—or even the better term *personal development*—is unbiblical or secular, thank you for continuing to read this. The Bible is full of practical principles that inspire better living. The God who created us and designed this life has a lot to say about how to make the most of our lives—how to live *life to the full*. But the Bible is not exhaustive. It's just a slice of reality—written at particular times and places—and we build upon its foundation for a more contextualized experience of present-day reality. I hope that this book is one more contribution to that present reality.

So when I say "affirmations," I hope you don't think *warm, fuzzy, feel-good guru*. And I hope you don't think Stuart Smalley from *Saturday Night Live*. If you do, you need new data.

In a recent counseling session, our Jedi marriage counselor assigned my wife homework. "I want you to do affirmations," he said. "You believe things about yourself that are untrue and lead to insecurity. And it's time to change your beliefs. That starts in your mind."

That reminded me of what I learned from Eric. Eric had me write down affirmations like this:

- I, Caleb Anderson, am a world-class communicator.
- I, Caleb Anderson, am a loving and thoughtful husband.
- I, Caleb Anderson, am loved by God and have his favor.

Nehemiah's people needed new data.

> Then I *said* to them, "You see the trouble we are in: Jerusalem lies in ruins, and its gates have been burned with fire. Come, let us rebuild the wall of Jerusalem, and we will no longer be in disgrace." I also *told* them about the gracious hand of my God on me and what the king had said to me.[35]

Nehemiah *said* and *told*. His words would give the people new data that would lead to a new belief: change is possible. We can do this.

Nehemiah provoked the people with his "You see?" I paraphrase: "This is the current reality. Notice. Pay attention. Can you see it now? You live with what you tolerate. And you are tolerating a sad existence. But no more. We're changing this.

"We. Are. Rebuilding. The. Wall! Imagine it. Envision it. Believe it. It's possible."

He painted the picture with words and declared that it could be done. Yesterday, the only thing people could see were burned bricks and broken dreams. Now, they had a beautiful future. And they were beginning to believe that it was possible.

Why? Because someone opened up his mouth and *said* it was possible.

USE YOUR WORDS

I have two boys, Jack and Henry. Henry is one year old and doesn't really talk. Jack is three years old and fills the air with chatter. Until he gets fussy. Then he makes obnoxious grunting noises and resists whatever it is that we're asking of him.

"Jack," I'll urge, "use your words. Tell me what's wrong."

More noises, fussing, and sometimes writhing on the floor.

Use your words. We can help you if you help us. Paint us a picture, describe the problem, say what you mean.

It's not only three-year-olds who need to learn to use their words—it's all of us!

How do you use your words?

We have a park across the street from our home. One or two afternoons a week I'll take Jack over to the playground. On a recent trip to the sandbox, I overheard a mom on her cell phone talking about her son. Her son was just a few feet away on the slide—definitely in earshot, and he was old enough to understand.

"He's a loner. He won't play with other kids. He's on the slide right now. There's another kid here, but he ignores him. I hope I don't have a psychopath on my hands."

Kids listen. They understand. They remember. And they—like all of us—are shaped by words spoken over them.

Statements like "He's a loner," "She's shy," "He's not smart," and "She struggles to make friends" become self-fulfilling prophecies. Words inform beliefs. Beliefs shape thinking. Thinking creates behaviors.

Make no mistake, words influence lives—for good and bad.

When I was in college, I read a quote from Thomas Carlyle that has stuck with me: "Tell a man he is brave, and you help him to become so."

Perhaps the statement stuck with me because I knew at my core it was true. It was about that same time in my life that I remember my dad telling me, "Caleb, you're an *encourager*. I see that when you encourage people, it impacts them—they believe you."

My dad's words influenced me. I believe him. I'm an encourager. I decided long ago to use my words for good.

NEW WORLDS

The first chapter of the Bible is a poetic telling of the creation story. Let me simplify it here for a clear purpose:

God said … and there was.

God said … and it happened.

God said … and it was so.

God said … and it existed.

God said … and it was good.

God spoke creation into being. With *words*. He said so, and it was. He spoke, and it came to be.

Words create worlds.

Next, God created humans to inhabit creation: "So God created mankind in his own image, in the image of God he created them."[36]

Don't miss this: God created you in *his* image. You have the creative gene. You're a cocreator with God.

God put the raw materials into this world when he spoke it into being. Now, you take raw materials like creativity, effort, and determination, and you speak new things into existence.

You are a cocreator with the Creator of the universe. It's in you. He's in you. He made you this way.

OAKVIEW COMMUNITY

When I first moved to Huntington Beach, I asked a senior official of the city about the biggest area of need. Without taking a breath, she said, "The Oakview Community." I probably looked puzzled. "You might know it as Slater Slums." Yep. That name I'd heard.

Oakview is one square mile and sits near the center of Huntington Beach. It's a low-income, high-density community with many immigrants, much poverty, and a high crime rate.

"The city has invested millions, and we've seen almost no breakthrough," she told me.

A few Sundays later, I stood up in front of our church and said with firm conviction: "We're going to serve the people of Oakview." The congregation looked back with similar confusion—the name didn't resonate.

"You know their community as Slater Slums. But not anymore. We will never use that term again. The community is called Oakview. And we're going to love the people and help bring dignity, hope, and a better future for their children."

And that process of positive change is well under way. Mariners is partnering with several other churches and nonprofit organizations, and hope is rising. Young people are responding. Parents are appreciative. The tide is turning. And we're just getting started.

Replacing the negative term "Slater Slums" and calling the community by its true name didn't change anyone's life overnight. But it did change something in our minds. And when we think differently, we believe differently … and then we behave differently.

Names matter.

"This is the name. And this is the future."

Words create worlds.

Words can bring death or life![37]

Use your words. Speak life. Speak a better future into being.

Lesson: You have the creative gene, and your words have the power of life or death.

Action: Fill in the spaces and blanks.

Words I have used that I no longer want to be part of my vocabulary:

Words I will speak with intention:

(Examples)
Vision

This is what was ... This is what will be ...

Encouragement

I believe in you. I see you as ...

Affirmation

I, _____, am a _____,

         (your name)   (who you're becoming)

and I will _____.

              (what you're working toward)

Visit FavorWithKings.com/affirmations for more help writing your own affirmations.

16

THE SPARK

*"If you aren't in over your head, how do you
know how tall you are?"* —*T. S. Eliot*

"Come, let us rebuild the wall." —*Nehemiah 2:17*

Jesus famously said, "Truly I tell you, if you have faith as small as
a mustard seed, you can say to this mountain, 'Move from here to
there,' and it will move. Nothing will be impossible for you."[38]

Why did he use the metaphor of a mustard seed? Probably
because it was the smallest seed with which his listeners would have
been familiar.

So what was his point? If your faith is in God, you need only a
little to see big results.

Without faith, you'll be blind. With faith in human things,
you'll see obstacles. With faith in God, you'll see mountains move.

When Nehemiah arrived, there were already fifty thousand or more people living in Jerusalem. Was Nehemiah the smartest among them? Not likely. Was he the one with an engineering background? Nope. Was he the best contractor? Doubt it. In fact, when Nehemiah showed up, his skin was moisturized and his hands were callus free.

He'd been a *cupbearer*. That's a cushy, white-collar job. What would make him think that he could spark such a massive effort affecting so many? It was simply his faith in the God who had given him favor and paved the way thus far.

I imagine Nehemiah looked around and saw what was once an impressive, protective city wall in shambles. There were tens of thousands of people living, exposed, inside that rectangular heap of massive stones, yet no one had successfully done anything to change their reality. And here was Nehemiah—with conviction, a plan, favor, and supplies.

"Why not me? Why not now?"

"If God is for me, who can be against me?"[39]

I'd encourage you to ask yourself those same questions.

BIGGER THAN US

Nehemiah became "the spark" for the Jewish remnant settling for a lesser experience of life, because he had allowed God to *spark* something in him. And that spark became a flame, and that flame worked its way out through faith—faith that the God who began this good work would carry it to completion.[40]

God uses people with passion and plans to spark great things, especially when those people remember that it was God who sparked a great thing in them to start. Nehemiah made sure that was clear, and the people followed him.

"I also told them about the gracious hand of my God on me and what the king had said to me. They replied, 'Let us start rebuilding.' So they began this good work."[41]

Nehemiah, in my words, is saying, "This is bigger than you and me. This is a God-thing! God broke my heart. God moved me to action. God gave me favor with a king. And God supplied me with the tools we'll need. If we fail—and I can't imagine we'll fail—it's still worth all the effort, since we believe God is in this. Now, it's go time!"

The people: "Let us start rebuilding."

A TURNAROUND FABLE

A business owner was deep in debt and could see no way out. Creditors were closing in, and no promise of hope was on the horizon. He sat on a park bench, head in his hands, wondering if anything could save his company from bankruptcy. Suddenly, an old man seemed to appear out of nowhere.

"I can see that something is troubling you," the old man said.

After listening to the struggles of this CEO, the old man responded, "I believe I can help you." He asked the man his name and wrote him a check. He pressed it into the sweaty, empty hand of the troubled CEO and said, "Take this money. Meet me here exactly one year from today, and you can pay me back then." Then the mysterious old man turned the corner and disappeared as quickly as he had come.

The businessman opened his hand and wiped his eyes. Looking again, he confirmed that the check had been made out for $500,000 and signed by John D. Rockefeller—then one of the richest men in the world.

My financial worries are gone, he thought. But soon after, he decided not to deposit the check but instead to put the life-changing piece of paper in his safe. Just knowing that $500,000 cash was at his fingertips might give him the strength to work out a way to save his business.

With renewed passion, focus, and optimism, he negotiated better deals and extended his debt terms. He closed several big sales. And within six months, he was out of debt and making money.

Exactly one year later, he returned to the same bench at the same park with the uncashed check in hand. Once again, the old man appeared. But just as the CEO was about to hand back the check and share his success story, a nurse came running up and grabbed the old man.

"Was he bothering you? I'm so glad I caught him," she said. "He's always escaping from the rest home and telling people he's John D. Rockefeller." And with that she led the old man away by the arm.

The businessman stood there, stunned. All year long, he'd been wheeling and dealing, buying and selling, convinced he had half a million dollars behind him. But it was just the funny money of a confused old man.

Suddenly, the CEO realized that it wasn't the money, real or fake, that had turned his life around. It was his belief that things were turning around for the good.[42]

This story is probably made up. But it illustrates a profound truth about faith. With faith, you can move mountains. In fact, Jesus also said, "With God all things are possible."[43]

Your faith is not in money or materials. Your faith is in the God of the universe who whispers to your soul that there is purpose and potential still locked in a safe within you—yet to be drawn upon.

Why not you? Why not now?

Michael Jordan said, "You must expect great things of yourself before you can do them."

You don't have to be the most qualified. You don't have to be the youngest, strongest, and brightest. You don't need to be first to market. It's better not to have all the money, fame, and fanfare.

What you need are conviction, favor, and a plan. And *faith*.

If you're waiting on God, he might be waiting on you.

If the problem still exists, and there are people still to be served, then there's room for you to be *the spark*.

Lesson: You don't need to be the smartest or the most impressive to be the spark.

Action: Write down all the insecurities you still have about what you're *not*. Now draw a big *X* through your list. At the bottom write, "I live by *faith*, not by sight." Keep the page displayed somewhere— preferably with your list of affirmations.

> *"Faith is to believe what you do not see; the reward of this faith is to see what you believe." —St. Augustine*

17

BLESSINGS AND BLOOD

"We have to pray with our eyes on God, not on the difficulties." —Oswald Chambers

"But when Sanballat the Horonite, Tobiah the Ammonite official and Geshem the Arab heard about it, they mocked and ridiculed us." —Nehemiah 2:19

Did you read the Nehemiah 2:19 quote above? It says that Nehemiah was ridiculed. He was made fun of, put down, laughed at, taunted, and tormented. All because he cared more about the Jewish remnant than his own creature comforts.

Imagine it. Put yourself in Nehemiah's shoes: "I don't need this. This is obviously going to be harder than I thought. Jerusalem is a mess. The people are a mess. And now *these* guys? I have to endure criticism and ridicule from these guys? They have no idea who I am or what I've given up to be here. And maybe I shouldn't be here. I don't need this job. I didn't ask for this treatment. I'm just trying to help!"

Ever been there? If not yet, you will be. So remember this: every great endeavor is surrounded by struggle.

There is a resistance in this world. There is evil. There are thieves that steal, kill, and destroy. There is darkness that light chases away. All good things endure an opposing counterstrike while this creation hangs in limbo.

God said that we have victory over the darkness because of Jesus, and that—later—darkness will be dealt a deathblow and God will make everything new.[44] In the in-between time, there is both blessing and blood.

As with weight lifting, being broken and beaten down by heavy resistance allows the muscles to regroup and be built up stronger. But the breaking down hurts in the moment. It feels good after— on the other side—but there's a reason everyone wants to be fit and few actually get in good shape. It's hard!

Everyone loves a baby, but no one enjoys labor. (So I've heard.) Everyone wants the blessings, but no one wants the blood. Yet we can't escape it.

RAILROAD TRACKS

Before the start of the new year, I went away for a time of reflection about the year ahead. I got the sense (I assume from God) that the coming year would be "a journey of blessing and blood." And that the blessings would outweigh the blood—but there would be blood.

The year proved the word. Personally, there was pain. I had a surgery go wrong, and it required a second surgery. The recovery ended up being close to a year. That meant ten months without physical activity. At the same time, Hilary and I had our second son, Henry. A healthy, hefty, sturdy boy who finally made his way into the world after thirty hours of labor.

Blessings and blood.

On the professional side, the church continued to grow, but we couldn't add any more services; four being our max at the public facility. Setting up for church at 6:00 a.m. and tearing down at 8:00 p.m. had taken a toll, not to mention giving a message four times in a day—every week. For over a year, we'd been engaged in negotiations to take over a movie theater, while fund-raising, and we're still yet to move in. We'd seen miracle zoning changes, financial gifts, and unwavering support. But there were also major delays, disappointments, and frustrations.

Blessings and blood.

I used to hear people say that life was a series of hills and valleys—some low times, some high times. In my life, I've discovered that, more frequently, life is like railroad tracks—one side is good, one side is difficult … all the time.

The interesting thing about railroad tracks is that when you look at them climbing into the distance, the two sides converge and visually present themselves as one. Such is life. The good and difficult converge with a long-term perspective and can been seen as one poetic movement telling the story of your life.

This is especially true when you look backward at the journey you've traveled. You see blessings and blood converging into one path. The hardest seasons of your life built the foundation for the good times that you were able to enjoy all the more because of the struggle to get there. Blood reminds you that character is refined through fire, progress is built through pain, and life is precious, not to be taken for granted.

Blessings and blood. Both, mysteriously, working for your ultimate good.

We know that in everything God works for the good of those who love him.[45]

The apostle Paul wrote those shocking yet hope-inspiring words after he'd suffered incredible loss, ridicule, and life-threatening abuse. Paul had been the most devout of the religious, but he walked away from rank, status, and comfort to struggle in a mysterious mission of advancing the good news of Jesus—a mission that brought all kinds of pain with it.

Blessings and blood.

No great endeavor avoids pain.

If there's no struggle, it's probably not a mission from God.

RED T-SHIRT

In a transition season in my twenties, I found myself living in a new community with no job and little purpose. I needed a break from a life that wasn't working. Maybe I was "finding myself"; maybe I was losing myself. Maybe I had lost so much I didn't recognize myself. Regardless, I had been humbled, and I was open.

I remember talking to my mom and she spoke words of wisdom that most twentysomethings need to hear: "Why don't you stop focusing on *you* and how your life isn't working and focus on *others* and help them in their life?"

Our selfie-obsessed culture of entitlement and fame fast tracking needs a dose of mom real talk.

The first nonprofit I found in the new town was the YMCA, so I volunteered there. For one day. Then they asked me to take a part-time job to fill a gap they had. Week one, they put me at the front desk and tossed me a red T-shirt. A bright red T-shirt that felt like a highlighter pointing out the hard times I'd fallen on in life. I was asked to greet members, smile, and troubleshoot any issues that arose. And issues arose.

I remember constantly biting my tongue as hurried exercisers raced past, taking a towel without making eye contact or grumbling about some feature of the gym that wasn't up to standard. My face was often as red as my shirt as I dealt with people who I assumed looked down on me because of my insignificant role that had started as a nice idea but become a challenge to my self-esteem.

There I was, in a red T-shirt, lending my time to this nonprofit doing good in the community ... *and I didn't need to be there!*

I wanted to shout that fact. "I don't need this job! I'm serving you. I'm trying to get the focus off myself and onto others. I was a Division I athlete at a major university. I have a business degree. You're not better than me!"

I know. I had issues.

Ironically, after week three of eating red-shirt humble pie behind the counter, I heard about a spiritual emphasis this YMCA was quietly promoting. They wanted to engage their members on spiritual and mental levels—not just physical. I had an idea, and I wrote an executive summary that got passed up the ladder.

When I had worked for Rick Warren at Saddleback, I was intimately involved in writing content and facilitating spiritual-growth campaigns. What if we did a health campaign—spirit, mind, body—at the YMCA? I would write a study book with daily readings that would help to develop health spiritually, mentally, and physically. We could put up banners, host group discussions, and integrate the material into existing classes and programs. It was a huge risk for the Y, but nothing great happens without taking risks, right?

The Y leadership not only went for the concept, but they bought ten thousand copies of *Chewables*.[46] They ran out of copies, and we printed another two thousand.

Chewables was my first book. I was an author. But only because I took my mom's advice and was willing to wear a red T-shirt. Despite the fact that I had a poor and prideful attitude about the process, God used the situation for good.

Blessings and blood.

God has a way of working all things—the good, the bad, the humiliating—for *good*, when you trust him.[47] And when, like Nehemiah, you're willing to endure some pain (or ridicule, embarrassment, loss) for the sake of purpose. And when you have a hope that you just might be on a mission from God.

Lesson: God uses both blessings and blood for good.

Action: Meditate on Psalm 23. Circle words that you need to reflect on in an effort to keep a longer-term perspective through temporary difficulties.

The LORD is my shepherd;
    I have all that I need.
He lets me rest in green meadows;
    he leads me beside peaceful streams.
    He renews my strength.
He guides me along right paths,
    bringing honor to his name.
Even when I walk
    through the darkest valley,
I will not be afraid,
    for you are close beside me.
Your rod and your staff
    protect and comfort me.
You prepare a feast for me
    in the presence of my enemies.
You honor me by anointing my head with oil.
    My cup overflows with blessings.
Surely your goodness and unfailing love will
        pursue me
    all the days of my life,
and I will live in the house of the LORD
    forever.

18

STACKING STONES

"Success is the sum of small efforts, repeated
day-in and day-out." —Robert Collier

"The men of Jericho built the adjoining section." —Nehemiah 3:2

I recently visited Israel and its majestic city of Jerusalem. It was breathtaking to come through the tunnel and see a big, bold, beautiful city that has existed through an Old Testament, a New Testament, and too many kingdoms and governments to explain. Excavation in and around Jerusalem is ongoing, and archaeologists are uncovering ancient ruins all the time. Year after year, more proofs of biblical stories are confirmed and framed in stone.

When we visited the walls of the Temple Mount,[48] I could see and touch actual stones that were in place at the time of Jesus. That means that the stones Nehemiah and his generation were dealing with were a little farther out (surrounding the small city) and a little farther down, below our feet.

Regarding these stones, I want to make sure you're not thinking red bricks in your backyard. These stones were as long as a man and as heavy as a small car. The elaborate pulley and people systems necessary to move these objects are staggering. When you see and touch the actual stones, it becomes a little more obvious why five guys with hard hats and coolers of beer didn't rebuild the structure on a Saturday long before Nehemiah's arrival. It was a beast of a project.

JERICHO

Notice that the verse at the start of this chapter refers to the "men of Jericho." You've likely heard of the city of Jericho. In the Old Testament account of the era when Joshua led the Israelite army, Jericho was a fortress with a circular wall that stood among the clouds as if to say, "Thou shalt not pass."

One thousand years prior to Nehemiah, God told Joshua and his army to conquer Jericho. At first, it seemed like a joke because the walls of Jericho loomed overhead like a mythical structure. But God was serious. "No, really … go take Jericho."

God: "March around the city for six days, and on the seventh day march around it seven times. Then blow some horns and shout and you'll win the battle."[49]

Joshua: "Wait, what?"

But, sure enough, marching, blowing, shouting, and then— *kaboom*! The walls came tumbling down. The stones of this formidable structure that took unbelievable effort to stack collapsed in an instant, right before the people's eyes.

Since you and I are still referring to this story over three thousand years later, I trust that it was still very much in the minds of the men of Jericho who lived in Nehemiah's day and were commissioned to join the project of rebuilding the wall surrounding Jerusalem. I imagine this thought crossed their minds at some point: *Uh, remember that story about God bringing down the wall of Jericho because of some horns and yelling? That was cool. And easy. What if we just marched around Jerusalem's broken-down wall and played some music? Maybe God would build the wall for us, just like he busted the one at Jericho.*

I respect the idea. Work smarter and all that. However, my experience with God—through the Bible, my life, and the lives of others I know—is that he doesn't operate this way. God has built certain natural-law principles into the universe.

You reap what you sow. You get out what you put in. There are no shortcuts to a meaningful life. The same goes for building walls. There's a proverb I've heard: "A tower takes years to build but can topple in an instant." Truth.

We see it every day—buildings, businesses, and people's lives.

My dad has said, "It takes a lifetime to build a legacy but only a moment to destroy it."

It is hard work to build a wall. Nehemiah has some great strategies (we'll see a few more), but there are no shortcuts. You have to stack one stone on top of another.

I wonder if God wired the universe that way to help us appreciate the gifts of life. If you don't work for something, you don't appreciate it. If you don't pay for something, you don't value it. But what costs you time, talent, trouble, and treasure stands as a reminder of a great work—a marker of a beautiful accomplishment worthy of the sacrifice.

Something has value when it's expensive or hard.

Do something difficult. It will have incredible value—to you and to others.

START

And start now.

I'll never forget the words of my friend and adviser Terry Hartshorn when he interrupted a discussion about the strategy and timing of a project we were working on by saying, "You have to start to start."

In other words, "How long will you talk about doing it before you do it?"

Start.

You'll never be completely ready. It's never the perfect time.

Look for evidence of the things we've discussed:

- conviction
- favor
- plans

And if you have the backing of the people who matter most—which, at the end of the day, is probably only your closest friends and family plus an authority figure—then start putting plans into action.

Wisdom has its place. Waiting and learning has its place. Preparing, planning, and prayer-boarding have a place and are critical to success. But there's a place called *stalling*.

And the only way I know to stop stalling is to *start* the work. Don't wait for it to be popular and sexy. You're *stacking stones*! That's not sexy. But the only way to finish a wall is one stone at a time.

FOUNDERS AND SELLERS

In the start-up world, some founders (often in technology companies) are starting something just to sell it as fast as they can. They only want the big payday. They are motivated to retire by forty and live between beach houses. Own a beach house if you can, but don't start to sell.

Start to serve.

Start to add value and make the world a better place. That's the only way you'll be satisfied in your life. People who live for themselves are never content. It's not enough. God designed us with an inner mechanism that finds joy and satisfaction only when we're aligned with our creator and contributing to his ongoing work in the world.

Terry Hartshorn founded PacifiCare Health Systems, built it up, created its culture, took it public, and employed thousands of people before selling the company decades later. Bonus: he's one of the most humble, soft-spoken CEOs I've ever met. For Terry, building a great business required being profitable, but the central purpose of the business was honoring God and serving people.

Find your mission from God. Hint: use skills while seeking to serve.

Then start stacking bricks.

This is the path to the good life.

Lesson: Towers—and walls—take time to build.

Action: Reflect on your prayer-board. What stones are ready to be stacked? Is there an order of next steps that's beginning to take shape? Stack the next stone.

19

HOW THINGS
GET DONE

*"Things rarely get stuck because of lack of time. They
get stuck because the doing of them has not been
defined."* —*David Allen,* Getting Things Done

*"The Fish Gate was built by the sons of Hassenaah.
They laid the beams, set up its doors, and installed
its bolts and bars."* —*Nehemiah 3:3*

Nehemiah chapter 3, verses 3, 6, 13, 14, and 15 say virtually the
same thing: "They rebuilt the gate, set up its doors, and installed its
bolts and bars."

Five different verses, same statement. Why would Nehemiah be
so redundant unless he was making a point?

His point: *we had a system.*

There is a map of the wall identifying each gate in the appendix. Each gate was named intentionally (and intuitively) and served a purpose for the community in the time it was designed. Clearly, Nehemiah felt that the purposes of the gates were still relevant to his community—or at least valuable for their culture and tradition. So he paid close attention to rebuilding each gate from the start. And he used a strategic, systemized approach.

Don't let your eyes glaze over. This matters for you.

No great project is accomplished without systems. Here's my simple definition of a *system*: "a pattern of behavior that results in a desired outcome."

Dan and Chip Heath call it "scripting change"—where you clearly define the outcome you want and then the microsteps that need to be engaged and repeated to accomplish the desired outcome.[50]

Let me give you two quick examples.

First, my dad has Crohn's disease. At his stage and age, the doctor recommended one of two courses of action: (1) radically changing his diet by eliminating foods X, Y, and Z and eating a heavy dose of foods A, B, and C; or (2) starting a round of chemotherapy. Clarity. Here are your two options, and here is how you'd carry them out.

It wouldn't be enough to say, "Eat healthier." That's not a plan, pattern, or system. The doctor (and nutritionist) built a clear and calculated dietary plan. My dad's job—not that it's easy—is to follow the system, eat the food on the list, and avoid the food not on the list.

Second example: With the help of my assistant, Kaycee, and my wife, Hilary, I created a system to finish writing this book. Some people will tell you that the creative process requires inspiration and that you cannot control when inspiration strikes. They're wrong.

The famous writer William Faulkner is credited with saying, "I write when I'm inspired, and I see to it that I'm inspired at nine o'clock every morning."

Part of accomplishing your project or vision is viewing it as valuable work. It is not a hobby. It is not an optional pursuit for your spare time when you feel like it and aren't too tired or busy with the distractions of life. Distractions in life are *endless*. So are excuses.

Start stacking stones.

And *build systems*. Script the change. Create a plan of action. Formulate patterns worth repeating.

Do the work. Rinse. Repeat. Continue chipping away and making progress until you're finished or until it becomes obvious you need to tweak your system.

DON'T BE A STATISTIC

Most well-meaning dreamers don't put legs to their visions and never end up accomplishing their dream projects. And most who do, don't see them through. The reason? It's not willpower. It's not a matter of intelligence. And it's not about opportunity.

The reason: *they didn't have strong enough convictions to find and follow a system.*

Let me give you a glimpse into my system for finishing this book. I had already written ten of thirty chapters before I reached an agreement with the publisher. The contract dictated that I would have three more months to finish. Clear timeline. So, I broke down my anticipated number of chapters into ninety days. I needed to write a chapter every four days.

From there, I blocked out the time in my calendar.

Saying "every four days" is not a good enough system. I needed specific blocks of time when I would commit to the writing process. And with two young boys at home and a full-time job, this part was tricky.

I find that in order to get my mind "in the zone" and establish a writing flow, I need at least blocks of ninety minutes—and blocks of two or three hours are better. So the question becomes, where can I find these blocks of time in my week? Early morning and evenings are my only options.

Early mornings are tough because my boys—Jack and Henry— both wake up at 6:00 a.m. (as if they've conspired during the night). I'm more of a morning person, but I'm not waking up at 4:00 a.m. on purpose. To write in the morning has meant leaving the house at 7:00 a.m. in order to get sixty to ninety minutes of writing done at the office before my other work-related priorities take over my day. We hired a babysitter to come to the house one day a week at 7:00 a.m. so I could go to the office and write while my wife was teaching Pilates at her studio.

Systems always cost something. They demand sacrifices—of time and/or money.

Evenings became the more consistent time blocks. The boys go to bed by 7:00 p.m., and my wife teaches Pilates early mornings, so she's in bed by 9:00 p.m. That means I can work from 8:30 p.m. until 10:00 or 11:00 p.m. without losing sleep and becoming unhealthy.

I blocked the time in my calendar and set reminders in my phone. It dings, and I go to work. ESPN needs to lose. Netflix needs to lose. My reading list—for a season—needs to lose. And I work hard to make sure the family does *not* lose.

The system needs to win, or nothing great ever gets finished.

Nehemiah created a system for the rebuilding of each gate: "They laid the beams, set up its doors, and installed its bolts and bars."

If you were assigned to a gate, this is what you did. You didn't do more things. And you didn't do fewer things. You did *these* things until they were finished. Then, with the gates reconstructed, serving as banners of God's blessing and construction momentum, the people moved on to other areas of the wall with a little more confidence.

Progress leads to more progress.

Defining a process leads to more confidence that progress is actually possible.

I don't know how to rebuild a massive wall that no one else has figured out how to build. But I can probably flail around for a while until I sort out how to *lay beams, set up doors, and install bolts and bars.*

Script the change you want to see.

How do you eat an elephant? One bite at a time.

Progress leads to more progress.

We stack one stone on top of another. And we create systems to make the work more manageable. Before we know it, we've made enough progress to justify enthusiasm and confidence that success is possible.

FROM BIG TO SMALL

Continue to define and articulate the vision. What's the bigger goal? What's your wall?

Next, begin to work your way backward from that future goal to the present. If you're going to reach the big goal, what are the smaller objectives that need to be executed to get there?

Systems become pathways to progress.

Define the incremental objectives. If you can define it, you can describe it. If you can describe it, you can delegate it. If you can delegate it, you can manage it … and you can measure your progress.

Create systems that work for you. Don't get stuck and become a statistic. It's not willpower you need. It's not a different family. It's probably not even a matter of quitting your job.

What you need are ever-deepening convictions and ever-sharpening systems.

And then you make a little progress that will inspire more progress.

Lesson: Creating and cultivating specific systems of work is how you get things done.

Action: Begin to design your next system.

In order to accomplish the larger goal, I will commit to follow this pattern of activity:

Action A: _____

Rhythm of engaging in Action A: _____

_____ (hourly, daily, weekly, monthly)

Time block for Action A: _____

Tools I need to accomplish Action A: _____

Action A leads to Action B: _____

20

MOMENTUM

"Without continual growth and progress, such words as improvement, achievement, and success have no meaning." —Benjamin Franklin

"The Fountain Gate was repaired by Shallum son of Kol-Hozeh, ruler of the district of Mizpah. He rebuilt it, roofing it over and putting its doors and bolts and bars in place. He also repaired the wall of the Pool of Siloam." —Nehemiah 3:15

I'm in the throes of early-childhood parenting. I love it, but the struggle is real.

To spank or not to spank? What constitutes a time-out? Absolutely no hitting, or is there a time and place for a good forearm shiver? Dinner the next morning if he won't eat it tonight? How strict with sleep training? And on and on we could go. There are more questions and experiments than sure answers or formulas.

However, I will tell you that at two years old, Jack potty trained like a champ! He made that big-boy potty his porcelain throne.

The secret sauce? Positive reinforcement.

We would remind Jack to tell us when he needed to do his business and how cool it was to keep his undies dry. When he would tell us in time and go in the toilet, we'd celebrate like it was his birthday. Cheers, treats, attaboys—the whole deal. He'd smile, give us a thumbs-up, and mentally tuck away the feeling of joy he got from doing this potty thing the big-boy way. He was potty trained within the week.

I realize I'm talking about kids and going potty, but I also believe that you've "grown up" too much. You and I are still kids at heart. You've got the potty thing down (hopefully), but you and I, both, still thrive on positive reinforcement.

Most of us know and understand the value of positive reinforcement, but I believe we tend to forget how effective it is as we age. We run into teachers and coaches and employers who are disappointed with their lives, hate their jobs, or just hate themselves, and they scare the smile out of progress. Growing up takes the joy out of childlike wins and new accomplishments. Personal development becomes "you ought to" instead of "you did it!"

We need less *you ought to* and more *you did it!*

CHEMISTRY

When I played volleyball at the University of Southern California, we had a talented team but a major problem—we didn't enjoy playing the game.

My coach was so angry that he made practice and games the low point of my day. I dreaded going to the gym. My teammates and I feared insults, cursing tirades, and running until we puked. Because we played in fear, we played tight and timid. Instead of uniting together against the opponent, we fought against one another. It was so bad that literally half the team quit after each season. Even though we had top recruiting classes each off-season, we consistently underachieved and underperformed. It was hard to watch, especially from the inside.

It doesn't matter if you're two, thirty-two, or sixty-two, humans respond best to positive reinforcement. We're all functioning with an encouragement deficit.

What's your favorite word to hear? I'll tell you. It's your own name. Guaranteed. It's science. And how much more so when your name is associated with compliments or praise. Praise is like an emotional vitamin, reinforcing your inner strength.

You need to understand this not only for you but for your family, friends, and the people you work with as well. You will not accomplish your dream, vision, or project in a vacuum. You will need to enlist the support of others—maybe one, two, or two thousand. But your progress will be linked to your ability to motivate yourself and at least one other human being.

Point them toward progress with praise. If you believe in them, maybe they will believe in themselves and act with confidence and courage.

Celebrate what you want to replicate. Catch people doing the right thing and throw mini-parties. People prefer praise to the alternative, and they're joining you because they believe in you and your vision. Celebrate that belief and their part in the progress.

Enthusiasm creates momentum.

CHECK-INS

On his hit television show *Extreme Weight Loss*, Chris Powell coaches clients on the adventure of their lives—truly becoming healthy in body, mind, and spirit. Most of his clients lose half of their body weight over the course of the year—some starting at well over four hundred pounds.

However, Chris does something genius that many goal setters completely screw up. He sets small goals.

He does not say, "This year you're going to lose two hundred pounds. Let's roll!" The poor person who has inevitably tried and failed fifty diet plans in his or her lifetime would quit before starting.

Instead, he creates smaller goals—goals that challenge but don't paralyze. Then, at each check-in, if the client achieves the goal, he or she gets a celebration. And the celebrations are awesome—international trips, lifelong dreams, meeting heroes, the works. After achieving smaller goals, the client begins to believe that total transformation just might be possible.

One day, one month, one quarter at a time.

Celebrate progress.

When I turned sixteen, my parents asked thirty adults—family and friends—to write me a letter about what it means to become a man. Then my parents invited a half dozen of these men to join my dad and me for a weekend away to celebrate my "passage into manhood."

Mom and Dad didn't feel like there were enough markers in life to help a young man see he's making progress and becoming an adult. They wanted to create a marker.

On the weekend retreat, Dad presented me with a folder of thirty personal letters—written to me! Each letter contained the author's most poignant thoughts about growing up, God, and how to persevere through life's challenges. That weekend, the men and I talked about their experiences and their encouragement for my future. It was an incredible gift. My parents and those adult friends created a marker for me.

You've made it this far.

You're well on your way.

You're special—no one is quite like you.

Keep going, keep growing, you're going to do great things.

If you want to make progress, pay attention to the steps. Create markers to celebrate how far you've come.

Nothing great happens overnight. Even the things and people who seem like "overnight successes" spent silent years in preparation. So how do you sustain progress through the painstaking years without any payoff? You manufacture markers and keep people motivated.

In Nehemiah chapter 3, verse 15 (at the start of this chapter), Nehemiah notes that Shallum rebuilt the Fountain Gate. He also notes that Shallum was a leader of a district—he had influence and was likely recognizable.

Shallum repaired the gate using the same system as everyone else: roof, doors, bolts, bars. When the system works, use it. And when he finished the gate—probably in record time, picking up on best practices from the other completed gates—he was motivated to keep working.

He also repaired the wall of the Pool of Siloam.

As I read the account of Nehemiah in chapter 3, it seems to me that the Fountain Gate was the final gate to be finished. Imagine hearing that Shallum—the leader of the district—knocked out the Fountain Gate in no time and then moved on to the Pool of Siloam. Not only are the gates finished, but an influential man in the community is so motivated by the work that he takes on the next project he sees.

Progress is motivating.

Make sure you and your people see and celebrate progress. When you see progress, you want to see more progress. You create believers. Believers buy in at deeper levels, and the project advances.

On the walls of our church office hang a number of markers. Photos of the team from years gone by. Flyers from the kickoff of that new service. A map with pins pointing to where our people live in the community we're collectively changing for good. These markers point to key events when people rallied, God delivered, and progress was made.

Something is working. Let's keep at it.

Progress generates momentum.

Jack wanted to keep making it to the big-boy toilet because it was obviously worth celebrating. Chris's clients believe that they can radically transform their minds, bodies, and lives when they see their smaller goals realized and the light at the end of the tunnel gets closer and brighter. Nehemiah created systems that generated "wins" and led workers to engage in the next phase of the project with enthusiasm.

People are hungry to grow, develop, and achieve. We just need to be reminded we can—that change is possible—and a brighter future is within reach.

One day at a time. One stone stacked on the next.

Progress generates enthusiasm and sparks momentum.

Lesson: Celebrating small "wins" generates momentum and more progress.

Action: Set a small goal. Throw a party when you reach the goal.

21

THE EINSTEIN OF DELEGATION

"No person will make a great business who wants to do it all himself or get all the credit." —Andrew Carnegie

"Above the Horse Gate, the priests made repairs, each in front of his own house." —Nehemiah 3:28

People work best when they care the most.

This principle is true for you, and it's true for people you need to accomplish the vision. And you need other people to accomplish whatever vision or project is in front of you.

That, of course, means that you'll want to improve your ability to influence others. Another term for this is *leadership*, but the term might be overused and abused today in our culture.

For-profit, not-for-profit, faith-based, corporate institutions—everyone wants to make you a leader. But there's one problem. Most people don't view themselves as leaders. That's why we are two-thirds of the way through this book and I haven't used the word *leadership* until this chapter. You might be one of those who defers leadership or doesn't think it's for you or would prefer to get out of it and not have the extra burden of responsibility if at all possible.

Yet you have a purpose for living. And you already influence *somebody*.

You have a mission from God. And that mission involves serving others and serving alongside others. We are inseparably connected to other humans on this shared, round playground. And cooperation is the key to any great project.

Instead of worrying about your level of leadership, let's just agree that you're going to need to work with people to accomplish a great thing. If you have the vision, the conviction, the favor, and a plan, at some point you're going to pass your passion on to others so the vision can reach its full potential. This chapter is about that.

SIMPLE DELEGATION

Don't overthink this.

You're about to see that Nehemiah is the Einstein of delegation and that his method of influencing others is straightforward yet genius.

"The priests made repairs, *each in front of his own house*."

People work best when they care the most.

So what did Nehemiah do? Pay attention; this could change the way you think about leadership.

Nehemiah assigned everyone to work on the parts of the wall that were the closest to their own homes!

That's it. That was his fundamental strategy.

More specifically, Nehemiah

- cultivated a belief among the people that the project was possible,
- showed them that God's favor was with them,
- provided the resources necessary for the work, and
- offered a system for the work, starting with the gates.

And then he empowered people to work nearest their own homes.

Think about it. If you know you're working on the part of the wall that protects your home and your family, how focused would you be? How conscientious? I'll tell you. You would *not* cut corners. You would definitely follow the best practices and systems that work. And you would work with speed and diligence until your section of the wall was finished. You would also work together with your neighbors to be certain that your portion integrated well with their portion. After all, you would not tolerate any gaps or inconsistencies in that part of the wall. Your home—your family—is at stake.

People work best when they care the most.

LIVING IN YOUR OWN HEAD

This principle is part of building conviction in the first place. Remember, you had a journey to get to this point. You had experiences, saw injustices, lived through pain, discovered your strengths and weaknesses, enjoyed wins, suffered losses, received a vision, discerned a path, took first steps … all to get you here—right now.

But others haven't been on your same journey. And you're the only person who lives in your head. Nobody can read your mind. They haven't been on your exact journey, haven't walked in your shoes, and don't yet have your same convictions. That means you're going to have to appeal to what you already know *they* value.

You're going to want others to work closest to their own homes.

People work best when they care the most, and they care the most about themselves, their families, and other convictions they've previously developed along their own journeys.

Reality check: it's not about you.

Every great accomplishment is great because it serves others. I realize you're passionate and might eat, breathe, and bleed the work. As you build deeper and deeper conviction, the line between you and the work gets blurry.

However, even if you're a carrier of the vision, the vision is bigger than you. It's a mission from God. Others will carry the vision with you. The work is *through* you, not *for* you. It's for a "them," and you need some of them to accomplish it.

Get out of your own head and begin to think like them. Where is their home? What makes their loved ones vulnerable? What matters most and will most motivate them?

Meet people where they are. And ask them to work on the part of the wall that protects *them, their* family, and *their* passions.

In other words, find the people with a self-serving interest in your project and begin to help them build conviction. Invite them on your journey by showing them how the work makes life better for them and the people they love. Then build from there.

DISCOVER THEN EMPOWER

My friend Graeme is leading a charge to communicate to the youth of Huntington Beach that a life of purpose and passion is possible beyond the cultural defaults of surfing, sex, and drugs. Over two hundred thousand people live in this city, and a third of them are under twenty-one. There's no way Graeme could personally talk to every single kid in the next few years before they graduated and moved on. The wall was too big to build alone. He needed help. So he asked for it.

He asked Julie. Julie already had a background of serving high school students through a particular nonprofit. She has incredible organizational skills and loves to help put plans to a vision. She was already passionate about students and building systems to support routinely engaging with them, so she joined the cause.

He asked Sally. Sally loves to cook, play beach volleyball, and lead small groups. Graeme empowered Sally to make treats for events, host beach-volleyball gatherings on Sunday afternoons, lead a small group of student leaders who would then lead a group of younger student leaders, and so on.

He asked Aaron. Aaron has a corporate job that pays the bills, but he is a kid at heart and loves to play. Graeme gave Aaron the responsibility of planning events for students and making them fun and entertaining—right in Aaron's wheelhouse.

Then there's Tessa, Lindsay, Jake, Mike, Megan, Holly, Ben—all of whom have stories about adults investing in their lives when they were junior- and senior-high students, and now they feel fulfilled when they invest in the lives of the next generation.

Together, they're stacking stones. Together, they're changing lives.

Each one has a personal interest in the overall vision. Each one brings unique passions and skills to the work. As the leader, Graeme discovers their passions and puts them to work in the place that hits closest to home.

Ask questions. Learn. Share the vision. Look for alignment. Discover what matters to a person, and determine if you're headed in a similar direction.

My friends Raan and Shea Parton started a clothing company called Apolis Global. Their motto is "Advocacy through industry." Instead of starting a nonprofit to advance social good, they started a for-profit clothing company with a huge heart.

Apolis Global makes clothing and other products with the highest standards in both quality and trade. They employ sewing shops in LA and all over the world, honoring their laborers with respectable wages, excellent materials, and great designs that command high prices in the marketplace. They shoot documentary-style videos introducing their international partners and celebrating the origins of their products. They put the coordinates—latitude and longitude—on the clothing tags to help tell the story of the real humans in other parts of the world who worked to produce each article of clothing. Their brand inspires the global citizen.

When it comes to vision, empowerment, and delegation, Apolis has it nailed. The generous wages they pay attract committed workers in places such as Los Angeles, Bangladesh, and Peru. Their commitment to fair trade and activism through industry appeals to a generation of social entrepreneurs and activists who line up to intern and work for this great company. And their designs and product offerings continue to improve, in part because of their commitment to discovering.

They send out a survey every December to learn from their customers. As an incentive, they offer 20 percent off the customer's next purchase for promptly filling out the survey. It works, and Apolis receives lots of feedback. And they learn ... and they improve ... and they know how to better mobilize their tribe of followers.

We're about to see that the people living in Jerusalem rebuilt their disastrous wall in a remarkably short amount of time. Yes, they had God's favor and blessing. But it's critical to note that God's favor and blessing came, in part, through the simple but brilliant delegation tactics of Nehemiah. He inspired a project that had once seemed impossible. He motivated a people who were stuck and settling for poor circumstances. And he moved them to swift action because he understood their internal motivations. He had them build the section of wall nearest their own homes.

People work best when they care the most.

Lesson: Mobilize people to contribute to the cause in places of pre-existing passions and bias.

Action: Build a method into your work for inviting feedback from the people you seek to serve.

What do you need to discover?

Whom do you need to learn from?

How can you empower people to align their personal passions with the larger vision?

> *"If your dream doesn't require a team your dream is too small." —Michael Hyatt*

22

NAMES

"Go with people who want to go with you." —*Kenton Beshore*

"Next to them, Zadok son of Immer ... Shemaiah son of
Shekaniah ... Hananiah son of Shelemiah, and Hanun,
the sixth son of Zalaph ... Meshullam son of ... Malkijah,
one of the goldsmiths." —*Nehemiah 3:29–31*

As the CEO of Horizon Air, Jeff Pinneo made it his goal to learn every staff person's name. They had a company directory with names and pictures, categorized by the airport city in which each staff member worked. As Jeff flew from one airport to another, he'd study the catalog of pictures and names religiously until arriving at his destination. His goal was to exit the plane and be able to say the name of any staff person he ran into—no matter where they fell on the organizational chart.

I asked Jeff about his practice, and this was his response: "No superhuman memory on my part, but a lot of intentionality and study. It's amazing to me how even five years later it continues to resonate. The following is from a Facebook post just this week:

> "'Jeff knew us by name and called us by name and asked us how we were and how our families were. A little bit of caring and respect and compassion go a *long* way. Thanks Jeff for all that you did!'"

Five years after Jeff resigned as CEO, people from Horizon Air are still posting on Facebook about how he made them feel.

Imagine how you would feel at the check-in counter if the CEO of the whole company identified you by name—without reading your name badge. You'd feel special, like a meaningful and valued member of the team. That was Jeff's goal. Because that's what Jeff believes.

Maya Angelou said, "People will forget what you said, people will forget what you did, but they will never forget how you made them feel."

Remember what we discovered in the last chapter: people are motivated by their own personal interests and by how their skills, passions, and priorities fit into the larger vision. That means that we do our best to help every individual *feel* like an important part of the work—because each person is.

Every name matters. Every person counts.

It's remarkable to me that in Nehemiah's memoirs he takes such care to identify so many people by name. The project is huge. The timeline is tight. The opposition is fierce. I don't know if I would have had the presence of mind to learn names and value each unique contribution. There's a job to be done, after all. Sometimes the individual is sacrificed for the whole.

Unless you're Jeff Pinneo. Unless you're Nehemiah.

Unless you're a leader who recognizes that every great work is accomplished for others and with others. And each "other" has a name.

WALKING AROUND

There was a slogan popularized by Tom Peters and Robert Waterman in the '80s called "Management by walking around."[51] The idea is that you get an honest sense of the state of your team, department, or organization if you're willing to set aside time to simply walk around, have conversations, and be available to people at all levels of your company.

Over two thousand years prior to Peters and Waterman, Nehemiah was already a genius manager. I know that because of his results and because he knew names.

He didn't have time to hire virtual assistants in the Philippines. He didn't have an Evernote app on his phone. And he didn't have an audio recorder to dictate to himself. He had to write things down and remember names—in his own human brain.

I meet a lot of people every single Sunday on the patio of our church. Sadly, I don't remember every name. I do, however, remember the names of the people with whom I spend extra time, have longer conversations, or make meaningful connections.

Stories stick. When you learn the story behind the name, your brain makes connections and creates pathways that lend themselves to quicker, more accurate recall.

I believe that Nehemiah walked around the wall and talked to the people. I think he knew them. I believe that he asked them questions, petted their dogs, complimented their work, and got extra commentary from wives and kids. I think he pretended to take a bite of a little girl's mud pie. I'm sure he had a tall glass of Mom's pomegranate lemonade while she joked with her husband about how her father was better at handiwork. He got to know the people who were dedicating their lives to the project.

The reason Nehemiah could recall and record all those names was because every name was a partner, every partner had a story, and he took the time to pay attention and value the person.

Every name matters. Every person counts.

THE FORGOTTEN

Then again, there are some who are forgotten—not because they don't matter, but because they don't participate.

Nehemiah doesn't call them out, but you know that there were some people living in and around Jerusalem who didn't believe. They were the doubters. Not necessarily antagonists, just doubters. People who opted out and played video games or stayed in their dead-end jobs, not willing to risk the life they knew—as limited as it was—for the life they couldn't be sure of.

Nehemiah doesn't condemn them. He just doesn't mention them.

The journals of history don't make room for the doubting cautious.

This is well illustrated in another story that has personal significance to me. It's the exploration of the land of Canaan.[52]

God told Moses to send a leader from each of the twelve tribes of Israel to explore Canaan. The fact that he sent one leader from each of the twelve tribes suggests that there was a decision to be made that might reach a vote and that the voting should represent the whole of the Israelites. In Numbers 13, Moses briefly listed the twelve tribes and their corresponding leaders, who were sent as spies to explore the land. Here's the list—read it; there's a point to this:

1. Shammua, tribe of Reuben
2. Shaphat, tribe of Simeon
3. Igal, tribe of Issachar
4. Palti, tribe of Benjamin
5. Gaddiel, tribe of Zebulun
6. Gaddi, tribe of Manasseh
7. Ammiel, tribe of Dan
8. Sethur, tribe of Asher
9. Nahbi, tribe of Naphtali
10. Geuel, tribe of Gad
11. Joshua, tribe of Ephraim
12. Caleb, tribe of Judah

In my Word document, as I'm writing this chapter, the first ten names have red squiggly lines under them. Word does not recognize those first ten names. But names eleven and twelve are understood by the Word auto-spellchecker. Those names are Joshua and Caleb.

My name is Caleb. My younger brother's name is Joshua.

I'm betting that you know someone who goes by the name Caleb or Josh. They are common names in the twenty-first century. Thousands of years after this story is recorded, only Joshua's and Caleb's names have stood the test of time.

Why? Why are the first ten names lost in the annals of history? I'll tell you why.

When the twelve came back from exploring the land of Canaan, Joshua and Caleb said, "We can do this. We can take the land. After all, God promised."

The other ten felt differently. They saw the size of the men already occupying the so-called Promised Land, and they panicked.

"We are like grasshoppers compared to them. There's no way. Can't be done. God must have meant a different land."

Because of their majority vote, the Israelites turned around and wandered in the desert forty more years. Because of the faith of Joshua and Caleb, their names endured throughout history. Bonus: they survived the desert wandering and eventually took possession of that very land promised by God that they had scouted forty years earlier.

No one remembers the doubters. No one names his or her kids Igal or Nahbi. They were part of the ten who didn't believe. They didn't take the risk. They didn't follow God's lead into the adventure of their lifetime.

But you will. And there will be others who go with you.

WITH

My friend Kenton Beshore consistently says, "Go with people who want to go with you."

In other words, don't waste time and energy trying to win over people who don't want to go with you on your adventure in pursuit of the vision. All the time and energy you expend trying to talk a few naysayers into participating is better spent inspiring the already motivated.

The converse of this statement also suggests that if people are willing to go with you, you should be willing to be *with* them—not barking orders from the palace, but working with, serving with, sweating with, and getting to know them.

Obviously, we quickly run into issues of scale—I can't know one thousand people intimately—but when you truly value people, it's obvious, at any scale or size. And it's obvious when you don't.

Every name matters. Every person counts.

Lesson: Go with people who want to go with you, and value each person.

Action: Walk around your place of influence and get to know someone today.

23

ENEMIES

"You may have to fight a battle more than once to win it." —Margaret Thatcher

"When Sanballat heard that we were rebuilding the wall, he became angry and was greatly incensed. He ridiculed the Jews." —Nehemiah 4:1–2

Enemies test your strength and make for good stories.

I wish enemies weren't a thing. But they're real. You can't avoid them in this broken world. Even if you're the most boring person trying to please everyone, you'll still find an enemy who resents that you're a people pleaser and wants you to take a stand for something. You can't win. Well, you can win, but you can't win with everyone. And some—because of their own stories of pain—are simply out to get you.

Every hero has a villain. Every great story has a great challenge. And to be victorious, you need opposition.

Enemies are opposition. Anything that opposes your health, your progress, or your people's health or progress is an "enemy." Enemies make an already challenging or complex journey painful.

No one wants to be targeted, opposed, or attacked. Enemies can cause us to question not only our work but also our value as human beings. Opposition can create chaos—throwing projects into turmoil and triggering deep insecurities on the inside. The bigger or more significant the work becomes, the more aggressively enemies advance.

My experience with enemies is nothing compared to people I know in other parts of the world, yet all of us encounter opposition. I've had people make fun of me—some I knew, some I didn't know. Others have felt I was being lifted above them and made it their mission to resist me or knock me down. Still others pounced on my lowest points and struggles to judge me as less than a perceived image.

I heard someone say that when you're out in front, you can expect to get hit from behind. And when you pop your head above the crowd, you become a target. Everyone deals with enemies at some point in life. And those who start, initiate, commit to, and lead great efforts are the ones who know the strongest opposition.

Nehemiah had three specific enemies. Their names were Sanballat, Tobiah, and Geshem. These men were from three different cultures that were displaced by the Israelites when God gave them the Promised Land generations prior.[53]

Sanballat, Tobiah, and Geshem were not just your average meathead bullies. They were each regional governors serving under the king of Persia. They had position and power, having been appointed by the king. They had influence with their people. And they had history—deep resentment that burned against the Jews.

In chapter 4 of Nehemiah's memoirs, Sanballat was motivating his allies and the Samarian army to oppose the Jews:

> He ridiculed the Jews, and in the presence of his associates and the army of Samaria, he said, "What are those feeble Jews doing? Will they restore their wall? Will they offer sacrifices? Will they finish in a day? Can they bring the stones back to life from those heaps of rubble—burned as they are?"[54]

These are vintage enemy tactics that have been employed throughout the ages. Reread his words. You'll eventually encounter the same.

- *Mocking*—or "ridicule." This can make the person being mocked become quickly discouraged.
- *Ganging up*—talking with his "associates." People feel more powerful when they unite against a common threat. This can make the common threat feel more vulnerable.
- *Prey on fear*—"feeble Jews" calls out the Jewish people's fear that they won't have the strength to persevere. It reminds them of their past, when they were unable to generate the physical, emotional, or political strength to do the work.
- *Doubt*—"Will they restore their wall?" The question makes the Jews' objective out to be a joke.

"Are you seriously planning to …? You don't really think you can …?"

- *Spiritual jab*—"Will they offer sacrifices?" The spiritual jab is an attack on faith. "You can't do this. And God's not going to do it for you." The attacked can sometimes begin to doubt if their invisible God is interested or participating in this very visible challenge.

- *Effort jab*—"Will they finish in a day?" It's kind of like saying, "Look at you working so hard. That's cute. Work, work, work with all your might. Maybe you'll be finished by dinner." These kinds of attacks make the vulnerable want to ease off, play it cool, and not look like they are trying so hard. As a result, the victim doesn't give the work his best. He'd rather look cool than desperate or determined.

- *Impossibility*—"Can they bring the stones back to life?" Another way of asking the same question is, "Do you see how impossible and stupid this is?" Here the enemy dramatizes the effort to make it seem even more ridiculous than it really is. "Back to life … heaps of rubble … burned." They use dramatic language to further discourage and make the project sound impossible. This approach can make a worker who's already questioning the work decide it really is impossible and give up.

Have you encountered attacks like these? If you haven't yet, you will.

Nehemiah's enemies are flesh and blood, with sticks and stones and words that harm. These are *overt* enemies. Perhaps even more dangerous and common are *covert* enemies. They may not scream and wave their hands. Instead, they may attack like a subtle cancer.

Either way, Nehemiah's example of dealing with an enemy can serve you. Here are three observations.

1. PAY ATTENTION

It's easy to get caught in the work or caught in the worry. Either way, you risk being oblivious to what's happening around you. Nehemiah pays attention and meets his enemy head on.

The enemies who are loud, obnoxious, and overt are exhausting and annoying, but they are seldom lethal. You see them for what they are and can protect against their schemes. It's the silent, sneaking, creeping enemies that threaten to do the most damage.

> Also our enemies said, "Before they know it or see
> us, we will be right there among them and will kill
> them and put an end to the work."[55]

It's difficult to defend against that which you do not see. Like a crouching lion, a stealthy enemy is subtle and seizes opportunities of unsuspecting victims.

Nehemiah took drastic action to protect the people and the project against a very real enemy. Your enemies may or may not have flesh and blood, but I assure you, they are quite real. So pay attention.

I remember when I was sixteen telling my mom she could trust me to drive myself around town. "I do trust you," Mom said. "I just don't trust the other drivers out there. You need to be a *defensive driver.*"

She was right. Now that I have kids of my own and live in Southern California with millions of crazy texting drivers, I see that defensive driving is the only rational way.

Pay attention to what's happening around you. Just because you're doing the right things doesn't mean they are.

In business, consultants can earn themselves a healthy living for the services they provide their clients. Sometimes you need an outside perspective to see the inside vulnerabilities.

That's the reason my wife and I see a marriage counselor on occasion—not because the wheels are coming off and we're in a state of emergency, but because there are enemies we see and those we don't. We visit a counselor to help us pay attention.

Pay attention to where you're vulnerable. And be willing to pay for help to see what might be hidden and crouching in the shadows.

2. POSITION PROTECTION

Nehemiah paid attention, and then he positioned protection.

> Therefore I stationed some of the people behind the
> lowest points of the wall at the exposed places....
> I looked things over.... From that day on, half of
> my men did the work, while the other half were
> equipped with spears, shields, bows and armor.[56]

Once you identify the "exposed places," position guards there. And there *are* exposed places. Every good work has vulnerabilities, and they probably reflect your own personal weakness.

To locate your weaknesses, just start with your strengths. Strengths and weaknesses are opposites on the same coin. Your greatest weaknesses are usually the flip side of your greatest strengths.

For example, if you are a driven achiever, constantly reading, planning, and improving, that's a wondering strength. Your weakness will likely be that you have trouble living in the present and appreciating the small victories and joys of today.

That particular weakness makes you vulnerable to stress, being disconnected from the people you're with, and making those closest to you—and those who work for you—feel like they are never good enough. That is where a covert, subtle enemy would attack. Overt enemies would aggressively compete against you because your drive and success make *them* feel insecure.

Know your weaknesses and guard against the vulnerability.

Unlike our Jewish builders, it's unlikely you'll need spears, nunchakus, and bow staffs to protect your efforts. But you'll need something. You'll need something practical, something physical—like hiring people whose strengths complement your weaknesses. And more importantly, you'll need spiritual protection.

3. FIGHT SPIRITUAL BATTLES

This side of heaven, there will always be resistance to progress. Jesus said, "In this world you will have trouble. But take heart! I have overcome the world."[57]

The resistance will come through circumstances, sickness, setbacks, bureaucracy, and individual people opposed to your progress. But it's never really about the people.

> For we are not fighting against flesh-and-blood
> enemies, but against evil rulers and authorities of the
> unseen world, against mighty powers in this dark
> world, and against evil spirits in the heavenly places.[58]

It's difficult to discuss unseen powers or evil spirits. They are otherworldly yet have some sort of influence in this world.

There are two sides you can fall off when it comes to unseen evil forces: (1) you can ignore them; or (2) you can obsess about them. Both paths are unhelpful. If you ignore evil, your ignorance could be costly. It's possible that a single invisible prayer could have had a tangible impact. However, it's also possible to obsess about the dark world and see the devil in every stubbed toe. That would preoccupy you and make you socially awkward.

The general outlook I live by is, *pray as you go—but go!*

Prayers of action:

- "God, protect us from evil and give us favor with kings. Use us to advance the cause."
- "God, you are the King of all kings. I submit my efforts to you again today. Now, it's time to get to work."
- "God, if you aren't in this, I want no part of it. Guide us, protect us, give us strength for the task at hand."

Enemies are real. But they are more spiritual than physical. Fight spiritual battles with spiritual weapons. In other words, *pray*.

Light overcomes darkness—always ... eventually.

Lesson: Expect visible and invisible opposition and defend against it.

Action: Guard against enemies:

Overt

My biggest strengths:

1. _____

2. _____

The corresponding weaknesses:

1. _____

2. _____

I will, practically, guard myself and the work against these weaknesses by:

Covert

Pray for spiritual protection as part of your daily routine. Turn one of my prayers of action into your daily mantra. Say it with regularity. Make the words fit you, and write them down here:

24

EYES UP

"I lift up my eyes to the mountains—where does my help
come from? My help comes from the Lord, the Maker of
heaven and earth." —David (Psalm 121:1–2)

"Meanwhile, the people in Judah said, 'The strength of
the laborers is giving out, and there is so much rubble that
we cannot rebuild the wall.'" —Nehemiah 4:10

When you focus on the problems, discouragement is inevitable.
When you focus on the possibilities, you become nearly unstoppable.

Sanballat and the other enemies of the Jews had just been ridicul-
ing the people for working on the wall. They were doing everything
they could to intimidate the workers and put an end to the project.
Nehemiah knew how fragile momentum could be, and he was ner-
vous about his people's response. He prayed, "Do not ignore their

guilt … for they have provoked you to anger here in front of the builders."[59]

In other words, "It's one thing to intimidate me and bring opposition to the leader, but to attack the faithful—the workers—is to hatefully attack the morale of the mission. Do something, God!"

Nehemiah's concerns were justified. Just a few verses later we read that the verbal, emotional, and spiritual attacks of the enemy took a toll.

> Then the people of Judah began to complain, "The workers are getting tired, and there is so much rubble to be moved. We will never be able to build the wall by ourselves."[60]

This was after the wall was halfway finished! There was momentum. There was obvious progress. And yet the people gave way to discouragement and doubt.

There's a clear cause for the turn of events, and it goes beyond the opposition: "We will never be able to build the wall by ourselves."

They took their eyes off the mission and off their God, who gave them the mission. Instead, they focused on everything that was going wrong and that might go wrong.

You feel small when you focus on the big problems. But when you focus on your big God, it's your problems that seem small.

The legendary apostle Peter learned this lesson the wet way. He saw Jesus walking toward his boat—on top of the stormy waves. Like a good disciple, Peter wanted to follow in his teacher's footsteps, so he stepped out of the boat.

Talk about an adventure in faith! And the story goes that Pete actually took a few steps on top of the surface of the water. I don't get the science behind this, so let's chalk it up to "miracle."

But Pete's miracle was short lived. After taking a few tentative steps that probably resembled the first of my one-year-old or those of a newborn fawn, Pete became acutely aware of the fact that he was outside the boat. Apparently, he had gotten caught up in the moment.

"Jesus is walking on water. I'm Jesus's disciple. I should try to walk on water."

Maybe it was like a frat guy leaping from the roof of a house into the hot tub to impress a girl. There's not a lot of thought or planning that goes into it—until you're in midair and consumed with rational regret.

The what-was-I-thinking moment hit Pete when he noticed how big the waves were.

"What was I thinking? These waves are as tall as me. *I'm unable to do this by myself.*"

When we focus on the wind, the waves, the circumstances, and the problems, we're not up for the task. We're too small. The issues are too big and complex. It's a nonstarter. What was I thinking?

But that's why we don't focus on the problems.

We keep our eyes up and focus on the God who walks on water.

PUSHING THROUGH

Earlier this week, I saw a lot of red *X*s on social media. People were writing an *X* on the outside of their hands as a symbol of solidarity standing against human trafficking and slavery. "End it!" they said. "Now is the time. We can change this. Join us."

They were talking about the twenty-five million women and children worldwide who are sold into slavery—sex slavery (80 percent) and forced labor (20 percent).[61] It's mind blowing. And it's unacceptable that such atrocities are taking place in our generation. But more and more people are doing something about it.

Numerous friends and acquaintances have invested heavily in the fight against human trafficking, especially in the past ten years. They have given money, joined organizations, and started new projects in an effort to turn the tide on this disgraceful human reality.

And yet, there are new articles, posts, and stats every day that paint a grim picture of the story. More crimes. New victims. New networks facilitating slavery. I visited Cambodia, for example, and learned of young girls who are rescued from forced prostitution only to be sold right back into slavery by a family member. There is so much more work to be done and so many battles to be fought that the outlook of global human trafficking could seem overwhelming if not futile.

"There's so much rubble. We'll never be able to …"

Unrelated to human trafficking, my friends James and Bryce just left their comfortable careers to start their own business together. Their other jobs weren't bad. James was making a great living, and Bryce was having a meaningful impact. But they both believed there was more. There was work that would be more fulfilling, more strategic, and more fun together. So they made the leap.

It's a scary jump—from certainty to uncertainty. From a paycheck to the potential of earnings. But James and Bryce had momentum from the start. They had customers in hand, and they did great work for those customers. Things were looking good. Then the circumstances got more serious.

There were medical bills. One wife wanted another child. One customer backed out of a high-paying project they were counting on. Cash flow was tight, anxiety was high, and James and Bryce were tempted to question whether this endeavor had been the right decision and if it was worth it to carry on.

They have carried on, and they are killing it. Our friends who fight against the darkness of human trafficking are also carrying on. Day by day, they press on and stay focused on the mission, despite inevitable discouragement.

There are countless examples of visions that are becoming reality, people who are all in for the cause and seeing momentum … and then disaster threatens the work. A threat is introduced. The wind and waves get really big. And even though we knew there would be opposition and resistance, when the stakes are elevated, people panic.

People panicked on Nehemiah. People panic today.

The question is, when people get paralyzed by the problems, will you get flustered and frustrated, or will you keep your eyes up and find a way through?

Nehemiah did several things to keep the project moving and the people from giving up.

1. He ignored the negative comments expressing doubt. Nehemiah recognized that when people are exhausted and afraid, they are prone to say stupid things. He didn't scold them. His lack of response was his response.

"Of course there's rubble. We are rebuilding a broken-down wall. By the way, we're halfway done!"

That is what Nehemiah didn't say. Instead, he did something much more productive. He gave them a way through.

2. He stationed guards. We talked about enemies and positioning guards in the previous chapter. Guards were strategic in two ways: (1) they created a sense of security—people were keeping watch; and (2) they gave workers time to rest. When you're on guard, you have to stay alert, but you don't have to move extremely heavy stones.

3. He cut out the commute. In chapter 4, verse 22, Nehemiah said, "Have every man and his helper stay inside Jerusalem at night, so they can serve us as guards by night and as workers by day."

This didn't mean that the men never slept. A man and his helper—literally, "younger man" or apprentice—would take shifts. The man would sleep several hours while the apprentice kept watch and vice versa.

And they stayed within the rising walls of Jerusalem instead of going home each night (many lived in houses outside the city walls). They missed their families, but they preserved time and energy by not walking the distance home and back each day. Sacrifices like that are possible in short-term stints, and they help build community and momentum.

4. He valued mentoring. Nehemiah clearly affirmed the significant role of the younger men, or apprentices. This points to a much bigger principle: Empowering a younger person boosts morale and gives energy. The younger person feels believed in, and the mentor receives support.

BATTERIES

The point about mentoring brings me to one final thought: recruit people for your cause who come with their own batteries.

By batteries, I mean that they understand energy and can recharge themselves without needing you to continually fill their tanks or motivate them. The opposite are "needy" people.

If time is your most valuable asset, *energy* is the bank that protects it.

Learn to manage your energy. When you manage energy, "the strength of the laborers" doesn't give out.

Beyond eating right, sleeping enough, and avoiding activities that drain you, the best way to increase your energy is to surround yourself with people who energize you. It's intuitive, but you probably aren't being intentional about it.

Maximize time with people who fuel you, and minimize time with people who drain you. Some people need extra grace and are just part of your life. Love them too. Just make sure you're allowing yourself to be filled up and not just poured out.

Therefore, when it comes to your project at hand, don't jump at the first person with a pulse who is willing to carry stones. Serve the masses, but be selective with your team. Do whatever you can to work with people who come with their own batteries. People who are self-motivated make the greatest teammates and employees.

I am grateful that the staff of Mariners Church are a joy to work with. Most days, I walk out of my office to smiling faces filled with purpose, hope, and optimism.

The general environment they help create feels like:

"We *get* to do this!"

"Let's make it even better."

"God is good, all the time."

Do your best to work with energized people. Maintain energy and momentum by keeping your eyes up—above the waves and on the God who walks on water.

Lesson: Keep your eyes above the problems and on God.

Action: Schedule time this week with someone who gives you energy.

25

THE GOOD FIGHT

"The revolution is still on." —*Os Guinness*

"Don't be afraid of them. Remember the Lord, who is great and awesome, and fight for your families." —*Nehemiah 4:14*

Years ago, I did a gorilla trek in the hills connecting Rwanda and the Congo. Guides escorted our group with rifles through the dense African forest. The guides spoke to one another in their native tongue and on radios, coordinating their efforts and trying to ensure that our group got to see gorillas. We didn't have to walk long before we came upon a family of gorillas relaxing in a meadow. The gorillas knew we were there and didn't seem to care. The guides weren't especially engaged themselves. Apparently, four-hundred-pound silverback gorillas are commonplace in the jungles of Africa. I was both in awe and a sweaty mess. I watched from a not-so-safe distance as a gorilla strolled through his habitat, effortlessly snapping thin tree trunks with a single hand.

It was amazing. Our proximity to these incredible beasts—in their home, on their terms—was exhilarating, and remarkably dangerous.

Everything was fine until a woman in her late twenties—Kate—got too focused on her pseudo-Nat-Geo photography and crossed a line. She unknowingly walked between an enormous mama gorilla and her child. Before any of us understood what had happened, the mama gorilla beat her chest—yes, she beat her chest—and bolted in Kate's direction.

Now, this could have gone on *Faces of Death*. I had just seen strolling gorillas snapping tree trunks far thicker than human bones. But the mama gorilla wasn't looking to kill—just to scare. She came at Kate faster than any of us imagined possible. But instead of mauling or hand fighting, the mama gorilla simply pushed past our friend on her way to her baby, giving Kate a forearm shiver she'd remember the rest of her life. Lives were spared, but the point was clear.

You can invade my habitat. You can point, stare, and snap your photos. But don't ever come between me and my family.

Point taken.

The gorilla was clear about what was and what wasn't worth fighting for.

Are you?

THE REVOLUTION

A number of years ago, I was invited to spend a long weekend with a dozen or so twentysomething up-and-comers (whose résumés were far more impressive than mine) on the Chesapeake Bay. There were a few mentor types with us who passed on wisdom from their journeys. One of those men was Os Guinness.

Os is an author and social critic who has written or edited thirty books. He is a man of great wisdom and insight, yet he is incredibly humble and unassuming. But on this occasion, it wasn't Os's insightful social commentaries that I recall a decade later. It was how he described one particular friendship.

Os talked about a friend who also was in a position of prominence—I believe in Washington, DC. Os lives in England, but once or twice a year, the two would meet up in a pub somewhere in a bustling part of the world to connect and encourage each other.

According to Os, "No doubt one of us would be wrestling with some struggle, setback, or discouraged about the trajectory of our work. However, refusing to give into despair, determined to never give up, we would always ask each other, 'Is the revolution still on?'"

In other words, for Os and his friend, this question was about getting their eyes back on a bigger story:

Is God still on the throne?

Is the resurrection still real?

Is light still pushing back darkness?

Is life still breaking through death?

Is the revolution still on?

If the revolution is still on, then we still have a part to play. Don't get distracted. Don't get discouraged. Don't succumb to depression.

Fight on.

"Don't be afraid ... Remember the Lord ... and fight for your families."[62]

In the face of the news of the enemy's intention to harm the people and end the work, Nehemiah pulls the entire group together to prevent panic and help them refocus on the mission. In essence, he says, "Fear not. Remember our God who is faithful. Understand what's worth fighting for."

FEAR NOT

I've mentioned the idea of fear previously, but it comes up again here because of the nature of fear—it's always trying to creep back in. You beat it once, you get your mind right and your faith established, but you find that fear is resilient. It keeps coming back, with sneak attacks.

> The Jews who lived near the enemy came and told us again and again, "They will come from all directions and attack us!"[63]

Fear is like a mythical warrior in an epic film. The defeated survivors return to camp and tell their commanding officer, "He was everywhere. He was on the perimeter, then he was right among us. He's like a ghost!" Take your pick of Mel Gibson characters. As the myth of the character grows, a regular man becomes almost immortal and unstoppable.

It's the same with fear. Fear is a five-foot-ten-inch man with male-pattern baldness who has you convinced you are small and cannot overcome him. He's the wizard behind the curtain projecting a fierce image, but it's all a facade. Fear is a dog whose bark is always bigger than its bite.

And fear's fundamental strategy is to trick you into freezing or flying away—so it doesn't have to fight you.

Fear will strike again and again, but you can strike back each time. Move beyond fear toward faith. You do that by *remembering the Lord.*

Remember his goodness. Remember his grace. Remember how he's always come through. It's been in his time, and in his way, but he always delivers.

Remember that he inspired this work in the first place. What God starts he finishes—one way or another.[64] Remember that he knew about your present circumstances before you started. He's not afraid. You don't have to be afraid.

Remember that he promises to never leave you.[65] He's always with you.[66]

Remember the Lord. And keep fighting.

FIGHT FOR ...

Fight for family. Fight for friends. Fight for people.

Fight for what matters most. And what matters most? The answer is always *other people.*

For a gorilla, it's her young child. For you, it might be your family, close friends, or people you have deep convictions to protect.

Fighting for yourself isn't satisfying. Living to please and provide for yourself won't cut it. Defending your own honor gets boring. But coming to the aid of a hurting friend, a marginalized group, or a forgotten people—now that will get you out of bed in the morning. That will keep your fire lit. That will inspire you and the people around you to great things.

Jesus was quite clear. When asked what the most important law of life was, he didn't miss a beat.

> "Love the Lord your God with all your heart and with all your soul and with all your mind." This is the first and greatest commandment. And the second is like it: "Love your neighbor as yourself." All the Law and the Prophets hang on these two commandments.[67]

Jesus claimed that all of Scripture points to these words, and this one simple idea.

Love God with all you are. Love people as you love yourself. And by saying "the second is like it," Jesus was suggesting that the part about loving others is of parallel significance to loving God. They go together.

In other words, love God by caring for others the way you care for yourself.

Simply to love God is a great start. But it's ambiguous. There's cop-out wiggle room. But "love others" has some skin on it. It shows. People feel that love—or the lack thereof. They know if you're generous with them or just with yourself. There are people who understand the degree to which you're willing to go to help them have a brighter future. You can't fake it. But you can fight for it.

Fight for other people.

Don't fight for revenge. Don't fight for ego. Don't fight for fame. Don't fight for finances. None of these things will satisfy you.

Stay clear on *who* is worth fighting for and *what* isn't.

And finally, fight by remembering the God who is powerful and good and the Source of every good thing. He is always with you. He's the four-hundred-pound silverback who's got *your* back. He's the friend in the pub who encourages you to never give up. He's the light at the end of the tunnel, the wind at your back, and the whisper in your soul to keep the faith … *and keep fighting.*

Lesson: Fight for others, and fight through obstacles, remembering that God is with you.

Action: Consider Os's example, and find your *person* and then your *pub*. Remind each other that "the revolution is still on."

My person: _____

My pub/place: _____

The revolution is still on!

Fight the good fight of the faith.[68]

26

THE MESSY MIDDLE

"A good leader leads the people from above them. A great leader leads the people from within them." —M. D. Arnold

"So we continued the work … Neither I nor my brothers nor my men nor the guards with me took off our clothes; each had his weapon, even when he went for water." —Nehemiah 4:21, 23

The enemy threat was real. The guys weren't wearing weapons in their tool belts for a calendar shoot. It was about survival. There was opposition to the work, and there was more work to be done.

But notice this from chapter 4, verse 23, above: neither Nehemiah nor his brothers, neither the key leaders nor the guards took off their clothes. That means they didn't stop. When they rested, they rested in their clothes. They didn't shower, shave, or sit in their recliners. They didn't ask anyone else to do what they themselves were unwilling to do. They worked shoulder to shoulder *with* the crew until the work was finished—right in the middle of the action, the adventure, and yes, the danger.

It's safer to stay at headquarters and send instructions. It's more comfortable to drive around the wall in your Hummer tossing out water bottles. But there's something special about a project in which the head honcho sweats alongside the frontline workers.

The natural, gravitational pull of leaders and people in charge is to allow delegation to creep toward isolation. Humans want to be more comfortable, and when the people we're serving become increasingly willing to serve us, the slope is slippery toward entitlement. We can appropriately talk about sustainability, and we've already proven that rhythms and healthy habits are a necessity, but there's a fine line between your personal health and creating an unnecessary hierarchy. And people feel the disconnectedness.

Alternatively, when you work with people in the messy middle, the people will work with you, and they'll walk with you—through fears, flights, and flames.

JESUS

Everything about Jesus surprised and astounded the culture of his day. No one expected God to restrict himself to a human body. No one expected this human to look ordinary. No one anticipated this ordinary human would hang out with regular people and reference the kingdom of God like it was a kindergarten playground: "Let's all be more like kids!"[69]

Jesus taught us a different way to be human. One of his great but subtle lessons can only be picked up by careful observation.

The instance I want us to notice took place while Jesus was walking to the home of an influential Jewish leader named Jairus.[70] Jairus's twelve-year-old daughter was sick and dying, and he begged for Jesus to come and heal her.

On the way, a woman—whose name is unknown—desperately bobbed and weaved her way through the mob of people surrounding Jesus until she could dive at his feet and touch the tassels dangling from his robe. When she did so, she was instantly healed. But the story isn't over. Jesus noticed that "power has gone out from him," and he stopped the crowd.

> "Who touched me?" Jesus asked.
>
> Peter said, "Master, the people are crowding and pressing against you." But Jesus said, "Someone touched me; I know that power has gone out from me."[71]

Don't miss this. People were crowding and pressing against Jesus. And he was okay with that! Not only was Jesus the most impressive, most powerful, most influential, and most famous person to ever live, but he was also God. And he was *touchable*.

Jesus lived, walked, and worked in the messy middle. He made himself accessible to the nameless who needed his touch.

That's how Jesus did his good work—*with*.

SERVANTS

While we're on the topic of Jesus, let me point to another crazy statement he made. A sentence so perplexing to his hearers, they could barely bend their minds toward it.

> Jesus called the Twelve and said, "Anyone who wants to be first must be the very last, and the servant of all."[72]

The idea of "servant leadership" has been popular in America for several decades. However, slogans and strategies are tested when things get messy. And that's exactly where a servant is willing to walk—in the mess.

Accomplishing great things is sexy only after the fact. Not during. The work itself is messy. And if you try to keep your hands clean, you're going to miss the most effective way to influence the work. And that's right in the messy middle of the action.

Monica is the outreach director of Mariners Church Huntington Beach. She helps mobilize the people in our church to engage with the poor and marginalized in our community. Within the city limits of Huntington Beach sits a one-square-mile neighborhood called the Oakview Community (we talked about this neighborhood earlier). In Oakview, the housing is dense, the crime rate is high, and the level of education is low. Our church has committed to building relationships in the Oakview neighborhood, doing whatever we can to make a legitimate and welcomed impact. Monica spearheads the effort.

Now that there are hundreds of volunteers who serve in Oakview, Monica could justify operating from her office through part-time staff and key volunteers. But that's not Monica. When she was just out of college, Monica went and lived at an orphanage in Mexico—for two-and-a-half years. She slept in a bunk. She ate what the kids ate. She went to the bathroom where the kids went. Two-and-a-half years. While most of her friends were starting careers and getting married, Monica was doing a great work.

Today, Monica could say, "I paid my dues. I did my time. I lived in a freaking orphanage! Now it's your turn, people!" But the past informs the present—it does not replace it. And when we see Monica tutoring children, handing out popsicles, or eating in the homes of Oakview residents, it inspires us to play our part too. It causes us to believe that maybe, just maybe, we can turn the tide in this community. Change is possible—one student, one act of kindness, one day at a time.

We need more Monicas, serving in the messy middle and changing the world one life, one touch at a time.

INTROVERTS

This is where some introverts panic.

The definition I use for *introvert* is "someone who recovers alone." In other words, some people get energy from groups. Others need to retreat from the group to rest and recover. By this definition, I am highly introverted. I gear up for groups, but I hit my limit and need to recover by myself.

But don't let being an introvert be your cop-out. Build in rhythms of action, engagement, and recharging. Leverage your thoughtful reflectiveness for maximizing your effectiveness when you're "on."

We need more heroes in the messy middle.

We need fewer pastors "performing" on stages and more giving hugs.

We need fewer directors dictating blindly and more with their fingers on the pulse.

We need fewer teachers going through the motions and more studying the culture.

We need you—*with* us—engaged in the work from the messy middle.

Lesson: Accomplish the work *with* the people.

Action: Do a personal inventory to assess how you're currently influencing others toward the greater good. Ask yourself:

Do those working toward the vision feel like I'm working with them?

Do the people who serve feel served by me?

Am I resting on activity in the past to justify inactivity in the present?

Are there any behaviors or patterns that indicate I have moved from delegation to isolation?

27

RAISE YOUR STANDARDS

"If you want to change your life, you have to raise your standards." —*Tony Robbins*

"So I continued, 'What you are doing is not right.
Shouldn't you ...'" —*Nehemiah 5:9*

Nehemiah had a practical but unrelated problem poisoning the work. And this happens all the time.

The closer the project gets to being finished, the more *other* issues arise. The people start to realize that a better future is possible and they begin to see the present for what it is—unacceptable. Things that were tolerable under the old standard are no longer so. Plus, a leader has emerged who has elevated our dignity and our understanding of what is possible. "We don't have to put up with the past injustice anymore. There's a better way."

The people brought to Nehemiah's attention that the wealthier nobles among them were making life more difficult for the lower and middle classes by charging interest for loans. Interest for loans might not seem like a corrupt exploitation, but consider the context.

The people struggling to make ends meet were struggling for the following reasons:

1. They were working on the wall. When you're working on a wall and not being paid for it, your family finances might get pinched. The wealthier seized this opportunity to make a buck.

2. There was a famine. Food was scarce. The families who didn't have the resources to store food struggled more than normal. Again, the wealthy were not generous and leveraged a famine anomaly for personal gain.

3. The Persian king hiked taxes. Don't get mad at the Persian king. He just paid for all the supplies Nehemiah brought for the wall. But the combination of fifty-plus days designated to working on the wall, a famine, and a tax hike were backbreaking for the month-to-month families.

Nehemiah was outraged that their own Jewish brothers and nobles would exploit their sacrifices and circumstances to make a buck. This was not a systemic issue of irresponsibility. This, in Nehemiah's view, was exploitation.

Nehemiah stood up in front of the nobles and called them on the carpet. "This is not acceptable. Make it right!" And, to their credit, they did. After all, it was a new day, and everyone knew it.

A NEW NORMAL

I've played sports my whole life, and I played on competitive teams through college. I've experienced how significantly a coach can affect a child's experience of a sport. Coaches can make or break the season. Coaches can cause kids to fall in love with a sport or run from it. Coaches have remarkable influence—for good and bad.

I pay extra attention to teams when a new coach is hired. In our world of lucrative collegiate and professional sports, coaches are on a short leash, and turnover is high. A new coach only has two to three years to turn a program around before his or her employer pulls the plug. The coaches who come in clear about their philosophy and methodology have the best chance of success.

A new head coach usually brings in a whole new regime—new assistants, new playbook, new expectations. They say things such as, "This is how things have been … Not anymore. This is how you've previously operated … Not anymore. We have a new standard around here. Embrace it, or find the exit."

That's what Nehemiah did: "There is a new standard. A new way of being human. A new level of respect and care that we'll show one another. This new wall represents a new way."

Turns out, the work was about more than the wall. It was about human dignity, being human, being the people of God.

This was always more than a project. For Nehemiah … and for *you*.

You are in the business of elevating humanity. God has high standards of love, peace, grace, and truth. You are part of his work—his standard. It's more than a wall.

INSECURITY

Nehemiah discovered what you will discover: People are greedy and controlling by nature. But underneath those behaviors lies a hidden, fundamental fear that has existed since the days of Adam and Eve: "I've got to get mine and protect my own without being exploited. I can't trust others. I'm not even sure I can trust God."

My friends the Hargraves adopted two boys from Nairobi, Kenya. The boys' mother was a drug addict with AIDS, and they lived in the city trash dump. The boys ate food they found or stole, and they took the edge off by sniffing glue and markers. Their life expectancy was in the single digits.

Imagine their turn of fate when a yearlong adoption process resulted in the boys getting on an airplane, which they had only seen in the sky, flying to America, which they had only heard about in the media, and walking into their own bedroom in a large house in Southern California. It was hitting the lottery without the taxes. They didn't know what to do with themselves. Baseballs, books, toothbrushes, running water, warm blankets—and meals!

Two weeks into their new life in America, the family was bonding and life was good. The parents were seeing the world through the eyes of the precious boys who had moved from the trash dump into their upstairs bedroom. And then my friends began to notice a peculiar behavior.

Mrs. Hargrave was helping the older boy clean his room one day, and she discovered several paper napkins and crumbs of food under the bed. She paid closer attention to the boys at meals, and what she discovered broke her heart. The boys were secretly sneaking food to their rooms after meals. They were hiding the reserves from the previous meal in case the next meal didn't come. After all, how could they be sure? They'd never had regular provisions.

It took months, if not years, for the boys to fully trust the Hargraves as providers. Old habits die hard. But my friends did the best they could to show the young Kenyan American boys that it was a new day—a new normal. They didn't have to be afraid anymore. They could always eat at their parents' table.

Fear and insecurity plague every human at some level in this broken world. Greed, arrogance, control, manipulation—those might be the presenting problems, but fear and insecurity are at the core. "People cannot be trusted. I can't count on God to provide."

Your project is more than a project. It's a new day. You're leading the way into a better future. A new normal. A new way of being human.

"Commit everything you do to the Lord. Trust him, and he will help you."[73] Maybe the greatest legacy of your life and work is about you trusting God, people seeing you trust God, and them trusting God.

You don't have to be afraid anymore.

You're not alone. You're not forgotten. You've been rescued.

It's a new day. The stones are stacking. People are working together. The enemy doesn't win.

Embrace a new normal and a higher standard. What was doesn't have to be what is. What was stuck doesn't have to stay that way. What was confused can be clarified. What was broken can be restored. What was corrupted can be cleaned out.

Raise your standard and let your life rise to the occasion.

It's always been about more than just a wall. Your project is more than just a project. You're elevating human life.

Lesson: You can raise your standard and elevate the lives around you.

Action: Define a "new normal" in your context—a new standard. Identify the old, lower standard you'll no longer tolerate. (Apply this to both your home life and your work life.)

We've been limited by …

We used to be okay with …

But now our standard will be …

28

SUCCESS AND KEEPING YOUR SOUL

"Try not to become a person of success, but rather try to become a person of value." —Albert Einstein

"I never demanded the food allotted to the governor, because the demands were heavy on these people." —Nehemiah 5:18

Just because you *can* doesn't mean you *should*.

Remember the movie *Elf*? It's a modern classic Christmas movie starring Will Ferrell as a grown man-elf who leaves the North Pole to find his father in New York City. His father is a children's book publisher, and in one scene, he brings in a special children's book author to get his team over the hump. On the phone, the author demands that he be picked up in a limousine, specifying the exact air-conditioned temperature of the vehicle, the food and drinks that need to be in the limo, and his fee for the appearance. He comes off like a high-maintenance prima donna, making the scene ridiculous and funny.

Recently, a pastor I know hosted a musician at his church who had some national recognition. He'd been on a reality television show that had thrust him into the spotlight. Today, he travels, plays music, sings, and speaks about his faith. By all accounts, he's a great guy.

When this singer agreed to perform at the church, his manager made a special request. He asked that there be a warm breakfast when his client arrived and also certain types of fruit in his greenroom. I thought of *Elf* and the author in the limo.

I'm a fan of warm breakfasts. I'm not mad at the guy. His weren't obscene requests. Still, it reminds me that every step up the ladder of fame and recognition humans ascend, the greater the degree of entitlement that accompanies the climb.

The more you get your way, the more you get used to getting your way. The more people you oversee, the more comfortable you become telling people what to do. The more recognized you become, the more you expect to be recognized.

That doesn't make you a bad person. It's just human nature. But it works against you in your pursuit of accomplishing great things.

Why?

The greater the gap between you and the people you aim to serve, the less you know about what really serves them. And the less relevant and impactful your work becomes.

Nehemiah understood that even though he *could*, it didn't mean that he *should*. He had a plan for anticipating and defending against what I call the "success gap."

THE SUCCESS GAP

The verse at the start of this chapter sheds new light on why Nehemiah was so effective in rebuilding the wall and leading the people. "I never demanded the food allotted to the governor, because the demands were heavy on these people."[74]

He could have, but he didn't.

The wall was about to be completed in a breathtaking fifty-two days, and in the wake of that success, Nehemiah indicated in chapter 5, verse 14, that he would become the governor of Judea for the twelve years that followed. That seems like a big jump from cupbearer. And it's definitely a significant leap from obscure Jewish guy who just showed up a couple of months ago from the Persian palace asking the people to take on a seemingly impossible project. Nehemiah climbed the ladder of influence and recognition quickly. Yet he avoided the success gap by taking less when he easily could have justified more.

There are praises when you're successful. There are perks when you win at work. And there's nothing wrong with counting and enjoying your blessings. But our natural tendency is to take them too far.

We've been disgusted when senators have exploited their positions for personal gain. We've been angry when investment bankers have given themselves multimillion-dollar bonuses for their performances fresh off a government bailout. And we're irritated when bosses take every liberty to make their own lives more comfortable while their staff struggle with day-to-day needs.

They can justify their benefits and their decisions. But there's something about it that just feels wrong. And there's something about those behaviors that forms a success gap between them and the people they intend (or once intended) to serve.

Elevation leads to entitlement. Entitlement leads to selfishness. Selfishness creates a chasm between you and others. Thus, a person's effectiveness in his or her work can eventually undermine that very same work. The more self-focused one becomes, the greater the distance between that person and the people. Eventually, his or her service is no longer the service of others but becomes self-service. And that person's credibility and effectiveness deteriorate.

Nehemiah could have lived more comfortably, but he chose not to. He easily could have talked himself into perks, but he wouldn't allow himself to indulge.

"I should park there because my time is more valuable."

"I should drive that because I can afford it."

"I should tilt this in my favor because I've paid my dues—and because I can."

Remember, perks don't make you bad. But they might compromise your influence. Indulging excessively causes others to feel left behind. Steadily increasing comforts take the edge off your passion for the project.

PASS THROUGH

Practice saying no. Abstaining is part of the training.

You don't have to say no to everything, but you'll want to say no to some things. It's a discipline that will keep you healthy. All in moderation. Any excessive indulgence is dangerous. So don't allow it. Decide now that you'll say no at least as often as you say yes.

The next time you are offered a vacation, first-class flight, large bonus, vehicle upgrade, etc., enjoy it. Appreciate it. But make the decision in that moment that you'll forgo something else. Look immediately at something else you can release and pass it through. Leverage a perk you could justify for yourself to bless someone who works with you.

Receive, release, and pass through.

If you need fruit in your greenroom, ask for fruit in your greenroom. But be grateful for it. Don't let success create a gap between you and other people. Bridge the gap by passing on blessings.

How could you make someone's day, week, month? What modest bonus for you would make a meaningful difference for someone else?

Release and pass through.

Even though you can, it doesn't mean you should. Keep the long game in mind, and make sure that the work continues to serve the whole—and not just you. This is the key to being successful and keeping your soul.

Jesus said, "And what do you benefit if you gain the whole world but lose your own soul?"[75]

His point is that there's a bigger story than just wealth and worldly possessions. There's something else happening here. There's a bigger mission. And you're part of it.

Look beyond the perks, and keep your eyes on the Provider.

Nehemiah was intentional about saying no in two more ways:

1. I'm not better. He knew that he was not better than the people he served as governor. He didn't inflate or elevate his status in his own mind. He came to serve the people, and he would continue to serve the people. Position wasn't important to him. Status didn't drive him. And the perks of leadership wouldn't derail him. Nehemiah was crystal clear: "I'm not better than them. We're all the same."

2. I'm not bitter. Nehemiah also refused to allow himself to become bitter. Keep in mind, he had left a comfortable position working directly for the king of Persia. He had favor with the king. There were plenty of perks in the Persian palace. Nehemiah gave up a great deal in order to sweat his face off working on the wall of Jerusalem. And it wasn't just about the wall. It was about the people, community, reformation, and a better future. But did the people appreciate that? Did they appreciate *him*?

That's never the point.

No one likes a martyr with a crappy attitude. It takes the sizzle out of the story when the hero is resentful of his sacrifice. But that wasn't the case with Nehemiah. His confidence was in God: "Remember me with favor, my God, for all I have done for these people."[76]

DEFERRED PAYMENT

This is important: Nehemiah's hope was that *God* would bless him, not that the people would repay him. Nehemiah's arrangement—agreement, if you will—was between him and his God.

Don't expect the people to repay you for your sacrifice. They don't understand what it cost. And if you try to explain it or make them feel it, you just seem like a jerk. It's not their job to understand it or make it right. It's not their obligation to bless you. Trust God to do the blessing.

"Do not store up for yourselves treasures on earth where moth and rust destroy … Store up treasures in heaven."[77]

Send your treasure ahead of you. Treasure doesn't last here. It's temporary. But if you defer payment to the next life, you can't lose what's coming to you.

Trust God to do the blessing, in this life and the next. And remember that the blessings aren't just yours. You're a conduit of blessing—they pass through you to and into the lives of others. God has and will continue to bless others through you.

Don't forget that when things work out and you're viewed as "successful." God is blessing others through your life. Enjoy it. But don't take the credit for it.

And remember that you didn't do this good work for the perks in the first place. You did it for *purpose*. You're on a mission from God. And you're not done yet.

Lesson: Receive, but be quick to release and pass blessings on to others.

Action: Take inventory of current and future perks. Make decisions now about what you'll keep and what you'll pass through and ahead of you.

Here are ways "the work" has led to blessings for me:

Here are blessings I can pass along to others:

     Perk: Person:

     Perk: Person:

     Perk: Person:

29

PERSEVERE

*"I do not think that there is any other quality so essential to
success of any kind as the quality of perseverance. It overcomes
almost everything, even nature." —John D. Rockefeller*

*"They were scheming to harm me; so I sent messengers to
them with this reply: 'I am carrying on a great project
and cannot go down.'" —Nehemiah 6:2–3*

We're almost to the end of our book, and this might be the most
important chapter you read.

Many intend to do something great. Few start. Even fewer finish. Those who finish are not the lucky ones. They are not the most
talented. They aren't the people who inherited the easier road or
more advantages than you or me. Neither are they the smartest or
most skilled.

The finishers are the ones who persevere.

There are countless examples of heroic perseverance in the accomplishment of dreams and visions. Every brand, all culture-shaping creations, and each purposeful project executed was saturated in both blessing and blood—sweat, struggle, and sweet tastes of victory. It's all part of it; it's a journey. Nothing good happens without sacrifice. And to endure through sacrifice and setbacks requires perseverance.

Victor Hugo said that *perseverance* is the secret of all triumphs.

Again, let this sink into your soul. It's not about being the smartest or having all the resources. It's not about being some fearless conquering hero. And it's not about some people having God's blessing and others being cursed. These things are man-made conclusions that dwarf the potential of would-be heroes.

You will do great things in your life because you will determine to not stop and not settle.

Sure, you might need to adjust your strategy. And it will never hurt to reread this book or Nehemiah's memoirs. And it will be critical to give yourself grace to fail while surrounding yourself with encouragers. But you will carry on. You will.

Do you recall the pieces of my story that I've referenced for you? Did you notice how intentional I've been about sharing my "losses" even more than my "wins"? Did you read between the lines when I shared:

My first marriage ended in divorce. I was a failure in the most important relationship in life. It wrecked me. But thanks to good people helping me reconnect to a good God, I discovered that "being wrecked" was exactly what I never knew I always needed. It turns out, you need to lose your life to find it.[78]

My first book came as a result of volunteering at the Y. It was an unsexy season of my life. There were days I was embarrassed, feeling like I had fallen into obscurity and irrelevance. Pride has to die before you can persevere and live a new dream.

My second book was rejected by every publisher. I ended up self-publishing, and as of this writing, with almost no marketing, that book has served several thousand people, starting at my church and moving outward through word of mouth. And it opened the door to the book you're reading now.

But this book almost didn't happen. When your first two books take hundreds of hours away from your loved ones—beyond your already full-time job—and net exactly $0.00, spouses tend to get a little skeptical about the validity of your next idea. And when a second child arrives when you're writing the book proposal, it's likely a deathblow. But my wife is heroic, and we persevered, together.

Yet probably the two most important ingredients to perseverance are *faith* and *attitude*.

FAITH

"Now faith is confidence in what we hope for and assurance about what we do not see."[79] Faith believes in a bigger story. That today is not all there is. That what you see in this material world is not the complete picture.

Faith believes.

Faith sees past pain to what's promised.

Faith compels you to stand when your knees buckle.

Faith guides you forward when you can't see through your tears.

Faith whispers, "It's worth it," no matter the cost.

Faith always has its roots in our mysterious connection with God. And yet faith is woven through every practical element and decision of our lives—and most of all, in your decision to persevere.

ATTITUDE

How would you act if people were "scheming to harm you" and you were already dog tired, working with all your resources—physically, mentally, emotionally, and spiritually—for the sake of a bunch of people who might not thank you or appreciate your sacrifice in the end? It would be difficult to stay poised and keep your wits about you. Grace under fire would be a tall order.

Yet Nehemiah is unwavering. "I am carrying on a great project and cannot go down."

He doesn't panic when persecuted. He doesn't quit when questioned. And he doesn't worry about himself or his reputation when rumors swirl. He keeps at the work by keeping his attitude up and his eyes elevated.

"Remember, O my God, all the evil things that Tobiah and Sanballat have done."[80]

"God, this is your project. I'm serving your people. I'm going to persevere and trust in your power."

When you become consumed by the complexity of your circumstances, your eyes fall and your attitude follows. But when you lift your eyes above the resistance, opposition, and chaos, you can persevere through anything, and you can sustain a good attitude no matter what.

Uncle Joe wrote in a letter to me when I turned sixteen, "The only thing you can control in life is your attitude."

I've thought about that statement often, and I've witnessed first-hand how true it is. Life is unpredictable. But come what may, you can bank on a future of peace and contentment if you can protect your attitude.

In both the army and his long career as an executive with a meat company, Uncle Joe saw his commitment to a positive attitude tested. But the ultimate test has come in the past several years as my aunt (his wife) Mona Joyce has deteriorated with Alzheimer's, a brutal disease that attacks the mind. Reasonable forgetfulness advances to the loss of speech, and the mind eventually forgets how to swallow or sustain life at all. Mona would forget where she put her keys or why she came into a room. But it was a few short years before she was forgetting the faces of loved ones and how to put on clothes and makeup.

Devastated by her deterioration and the progressing disconnection with his wife and best friend, Uncle Joe decided to keep a good attitude. He would love his wife well until the end. And he's had to make that decision again and again, painful day after painful day.

Knowing that style, fashion, and beauty had been important to Mona, Uncle Joe did something heroic that I'll never forget. He took his wife to her favorite department store—Nordstrom—and had the cosmetic staff teach him how to apply Mona's makeup. They went several times until he got it right. The foundation first, then this blush with that brush, eyebrows and lashes too. He became a student, dedicated to caring for his wife in this simple yet profound act of persevering love.

Uncle Joe gently, carefully applied his wife's makeup for over a year. He put Mona Joyce in a special home that gives exceptional care to people with Alzheimer's. He visits her every morning until lunch, runs errands and visits family members most afternoons, then stops back by to see his wife in the evening before returning to the home they shared for twenty years.

As I write this, my aunt Mona Joyce has surpassed her life expectancy even though her mind is barely active. And Uncle Joe … Uncle Joe has a joke and a smile ready anytime I see him. He still sends me articles about attitude—via the US Postal Service. (Makeup, he nailed. Social media, not so much.) And he still inspires me to love well and to persevere to the end with my head held high—no matter what may come.

"Therefore, since we are surrounded by such a huge crowd of witnesses to the life of faith … let us run with endurance the race God has set before us."[81]

Nehemiah led the people to accomplish the impossible. They finished the wall in fifty-two days. Yet when the wall was complete, Nehemiah's work was not done. He chose to stay with his people and serve as their governor for twelve more years. The work was always bigger than the wall.

The project is always about the people.

Nehemiah might not have realized it at the time, but he was being used by God to play a vital part in the story of the Jewish people, who set the stage for the coming of Jesus, who changed everything for everyone.[82]

You don't know how the decisions you're making today will affect not only your future but also your family, your friends, your neighbors … and maybe even a nation.

The project is always about the people. Not walls, not widgets, not wealth. You're honoring God by serving people.

Persevere.

Don't give up.

Have faith.

> So on October 2 the wall was finished—just fifty-two days after we had begun. When our enemies and the surrounding nations heard about it, they were frightened and humiliated. They realized this work had been done with the help of our God.[83]

There is a bigger story. Persevering is playing your part. And persevering is possible ... *with the help of our God.*

Lesson: Perseverance is more important than any other quality.

Action: Check your attitude. Don't get negative. Don't give up. These are the issues that are affecting my attitude:

This is what persevering in faith and with a positive attitude will look like in my life:

> *"Great works are performed not by strength but by perseverance." —Samuel Johnson*

30

GIVE IT AWAY

*"The function of leadership is to produce more
leaders, not more followers." —Ralph Nader*

*"After the wall had been rebuilt … I put in charge
of Jerusalem my brother Hanani, along with
Hananiah the commander of the citadel, because
he was a man of integrity." —Nehemiah 7:1–2*

In the past week, I spoke at my grandmother's memorial service
and at a separate event celebrating my parents' fortieth anniversary.
Reflecting more deeply than an average week, I made some observations about life and legacy that are also present in Nehemiah's
memoirs.

My grandmother died in her eighties after a life well lived. She
was the matriarch of the family, surviving my grandpa by twelve
years. The two of them were married fifty-two years, and for fifty of

those, my grandfather was a preacher man. Grandma raised my dad and his three siblings in dust bowls and trailers outside tent gatherings, sometimes feeding them with bags of beans my grandfather was given as payment for his ministry.

Eleven grandchildren followed. Five are pastors. All are fun, capable people who loved their grandma.

At the ceremony, we took turns sharing from the stage about our grandma and the legacy she leaves us. The recurring themes were:

- She prayed for us every day of our lives.
- She never forgot a birthday or Christmas gift.
- We never for a moment doubted her love, no matter how badly we failed.

In short, Grandma loved and believed in us, unconditionally.

My dad experienced raw and varied emotions—losing his hero-mother but celebrating his marriage with all three of his sons and seven grandkids. My parents are still in good health and going strong. Their forty-year marker is a rare and unusual accomplishment these days and worth celebrating.

Neither my parents nor grandparents are rich or famous, yet many credit them with leaving life-shaping legacies. And that brings us to a major myth in our culture: your legacy is about making a name or fortune for yourself.

Legacy is about what you leave behind for others. People who live to boost themselves will continually fight irrelevance and drift quickly into obscurity when they die. People who live to boost others will live on for generations in the lives of the people they loved and served.

Legacy is about giving your life away. You can't take anything with you, but you can leave a legacy behind you. And it's never too early to start thinking about your own legacy.

MARKERS

I've already mentioned that my parents made my sixteenth birthday a focal point in my life—a birthday more significant than other birthdays. They shared a conviction that "markers" are important in life, and sometimes you need to manufacture markers to commemorate significant events. I bring up the concept again here to take it a level deeper.

A marker is like a memorial, celebrating something that has happened, providing context for a point in time, and suggesting hope for a better tomorrow. Markers can make memories. Markers can set standards. Markers can help make paths forward.

My grandma gave me another marker. When I turned twenty-one, she handed me a "Grandmother Remembers" book. It was a template memory book that she diligently filled in by hand. It wasn't a twenty-one-year-old's dream gift, but today it's priceless to me.

In it, Grandma carefully, painstakingly, documented our family tree, recounted her own life—significant dates, memories, pictures—and moved on to my parents' lives and then to mine. It's a notebook that essentially says, "Here is your heritage. Now go and leave your own legacy."

Markers help make legacies. They help you shape, encourage, and direct people's experience of life. Without markers, we move through time and space with few handles for stability and fleeting reasons to celebrate.

Nehemiah leveraged markers.

He made a point of acknowledging when the wall was half-complete.[84]

He recorded the names of the families who participated in the building and who would live in the city of Jerusalem.[85]

He threw a massive party. Chapter 8 tells of a rare but significant gathering:

> All the people came together as one … On the first
> day of the seventh month Ezra the priest brought
> the Law before the assembly, which was made up of
> men and women and all who were able to under-
> stand. He read it aloud from daybreak till noon.[86]

Then Nehemiah said, "Go and enjoy choice food and sweet drinks, and send some to those who have nothing prepared. This day is holy to our Lord."[87]

It was an eat-drink-and-be-happy kind of day. Nehemiah under-stood the value of a good party. He created markers that would serve as a memorial for generations to come.

"God is good. Don't forget this. Let's party."

How can you create markers for the people around you? How can you make milestones matter and make people feel like they are making progress?

MEALS

My parents were big on eating meals together as a family. And they got it from Grandma.

Grandma always had a meal ready. Like it or not, if you're at her table, you're eating something—any time of day.

Holidays and birthdays were feasts. Thanksgiving was another level still. We'd snack for two hours watching football *before* dinner started. We'd eat dinner and then promptly pass out on the couch or floor, only to be awakened by a call for dessert—which was actually Grandma's specialty. These courses were not optional. They were expectations of a grandma who loved and served by providing sustenance for her family.

Humans bond over meals. There's something supernatural about the experience. More than coffee, more than a movie, a meal is intimate. When you're eating food, you're subconsciously aware that you cannot live without this nutrition. Your life would end without this resource. You and your dinner guests are in the same boat—vulnerable and needy, desperate for fuel to sustain life. Without it, there is no life.

Meals connect. They make a very normal necessity of everyday life more special when shared with another vulnerable human.

"Thank God for this sustaining nutrition. Without it, we would surely die."

Nehemiah leveraged meals.

> Furthermore, a hundred and fifty Jews and officials ate at my table, as well as those who came to us from the surrounding nations.[88]

Meals are a necessity. But they can also be a strategy.

How can you make the regular routine of eating meals more intentional, leaving a legacy by giving your life away to others?

ENTRUST

Let's pay attention to one more detail in the verse at the start of this chapter:

> … because he was a man of integrity.[89]

Nehemiah didn't give away his life and legacy to just anyone. Remember, he was incredibly intentional and strategic. He knew what he was doing. And he knew who was capable of what.

Nehemiah shared his life with some people more than others. Everyone got noticed, some were invested in, and a few were empowered. The men with the most integrity, who showed themselves most faithful in serving people, would be the ones Nehemiah would entrust with the most authority.

Jesus gave us the same model. He spoke to the masses, touched many, walked with a handful, and was especially close to just a few. Jesus also said something about not throwing your pearls to pigs.[90] In other words, don't waste your best stuff on people who don't recognize it or who don't have any value for it. Empower the ones who will steward the responsibility, using the blessing to bless others.

The project is in service of the people. It's not for you. And your legacy is not about your name being great.

Cultivate conviction.

Pray and plan.

Follow the favor.

Take the leap.

Mobilize the people.

Stack stones.

Persevere.

Then pass the torch to others who understand that we each play a small part in a much larger story. We are on a mission from God … for such a time as this.

There is a time and a season. A season for preparing. A season for doing. A season for continuing, despite opposition. And a season for handing off. Know the season you're in.

And don't tell yourself that there is no one you can trust to hand off your work to. You're kidding yourself. You've overinflated your role. If you can't find anyone worthy of entrusting the work to, it's an indictment on how you've chosen to work. You'll find yourself looking back on a legacy of self-sufficiency and not empowerment. Don't wait until the end to empower, because you won't. Practice empowering now.

Give it away.

Give responsibility. Share opportunity. Offer trust and support.

Sometimes people will surprise you and do better than you could have done on your own. Other times they will reinforce your fears. But don't pull back. Retrain or reposition, and keep practicing the discipline of giving the work away.

You can't take it with you. You can't lead forever. And the sooner you pry your grip off what is, the sooner it can blossom—even multiply—into what could be.

This has never been yours in the first place. It began as a mission from God. And it will always and ultimately be his.

Play your role. Then hand it off. It's bigger than you. And there's probably another project waiting for you to cultivate a new conviction.

And the story goes on …

Lesson: Practice empowering others sooner rather than later.

Action: List the people in your life who you believe have promise. Identify opportunities you can leverage to help them grow. Give something away this week.

May God bless you and keep you; may he deepen your convictions and increase your faith; may "the joy of the LORD be your strength."[91] And may the King of Kings give you favor.

APPENDIX

FOR GROUP
DISCUSSION

See FavorWithKings.com/group for a PDF of this discussion guide.

1. Session One: Purpose

Chapters: 1–5 (*Favor with Kings*)

Overview: The story of Nehemiah begins with *bad news*. It's no coincidence that bad news sparks purpose and passion for the rest of us too.

Objective: The goal of this group session is to get to know one another, build some trust by sharing honestly, then look for common ground.

Leader Tip: Create an environment of safety and authentic sharing so that your group will feel more comfortable getting honest sooner rather than later. The best way to do that is by

- sharing honestly and openly *first*;
- not coaching or fixing others, just validating and affirming; and
- praying for God to intervene and guide.

There are more leadership resources at FavorWithKings.com.

Questions:

1. Who are you and why are you here? What are you hoping to get out of this book and six-part series?

2. Who is someone that inspires you, and why?

Group Reading: Nehemiah 1:1–4

> The words of Nehemiah son of Hakaliah:
> In the month of Kislev in the twentieth year, while I was in the citadel of Susa, Hanani, one of my brothers, came from Judah with some other men, and I questioned them about the Jewish remnant that had survived the exile, and also about Jerusalem.

They said to me, "Those who survived the exile and are back in the province are in great trouble and disgrace. The wall of Jerusalem is broken down, and its gates have been burned with fire."

When I heard these things, I sat down and wept.

Additional Questions:

1. What stands out to you in the passage above?

2. Why do you think Nehemiah begins his memoirs this way?

3. When have you seen bad news move someone to take bold action and do something positive?

4. In chapter 3, Caleb Anderson says, "God doesn't waste your pain." What does that mean, or what *could* that mean to you?

5. In chapter 4, Anderson writes, "Your past is telling you something about your future." What event, circumstance, or experience from your past is coming to mind? Or what parts of your journey have most shaped you into who you are?

If there are any other key points, notes, or actions from the first five chapters of *Favor with Kings* you'd like to discuss, share them now.

6. What common threads do you see in people's stories in your group? Where do experiences or inspirations overlap?

As you prepare for the next session, catch up on any readings from chapters 1–5, and read as much of chapters 6–10 as possible.

Encourage one another to do the action steps at the end of each chapter. As part of the group experience, you'll also be invited to participate together in one simple action step each week.

Group Action: Create a rotation plan for someone to provide food (a meal or snacks) each time your group meets.

Close your time together with a short prayer.

Note for Next Session: If possible, carve out two hours for your next group meeting.

2. Session Two: Passion

Chapters: 6–10 (*Favor with Kings*)

Overview: Before Nehemiah takes drastic action, he pauses, prays, and fasts. In other words, he puts his trust in God and cultivates his own conviction.

Objective: The goal of this group session is to help one another tap into personal conviction and passion. Half of this session will be spent in personal reflection and prayer. Save thirty minutes to pray, individually, and then another fifteen to come back together and share.

Leader Tip: Push people beyond surface answers to dig deeper into who they are, what breaks their hearts, and what they can do about it. Then move the group toward commonality and a shared service project.

Questions:

1. Has anything interesting or unusual happened since the last group meeting? Describe it.

2. Does anyone yet have the sense that God is trying to get your attention? Explain.

Group Reading: Nehemiah 1:4–11

When I heard these things, I sat down and wept. For some days I mourned and fasted and prayed before the God of heaven. Then I said:

"Lord, the God of heaven, the great and awesome God, who keeps his covenant of love with those who love him and keep his commandments, let your ear be attentive and your eyes open to hear the prayer your servant is praying before you day and night for your servants, the people of Israel. I confess the sins we Israelites, including myself and my father's family, have committed against you. We have acted very wickedly toward you. We have not obeyed the commands, decrees and laws you gave your servant Moses.

"Remember the instruction you gave your servant Moses, saying, 'If you are unfaithful, I will scatter you among the nations, but if you return to me and obey my commands, then even if your exiled people are at the farthest horizon, I will gather them from there and bring them to the place I have chosen as a dwelling for my Name.'

"They are your servants and your people, whom you redeemed by your great strength and your mighty hand. Lord, let your ear be attentive to the prayer of this your servant and to the prayer of your servants who delight in revering your name. Give your servant success today by granting him favor in the presence of this man."

I was cupbearer to the king.

Additional Questions:

1. What stands out to you in the Nehemiah 1:4–11 passage?

2. Why do you think Nehemiah offers so much detail of his prayer?

3. When have you been desperate in your life? What did you do in your desperation?

Prayer Experience (30–45 minutes): Don't panic. You can do this.

It doesn't matter if you've prayed your whole life or only when driving with your tiny, blind grandma. Prayer is nothing to be afraid of, and it's good for your soul.

We're going to practice a short, simple time of prayer. These instructions will guide you through it.

Get alone, by yourself. (That means *not* with someone else.)

Keep the book open and on these instructions. If you're reading this digitally, use a journal also, or grab a notecard—Evernote works too.

Ask God to speak to you. Say something like, "Here I am, God. I'm open to whatever you might say to me."

You'll likely find that your mind will wander. That doesn't mean you're a bad person or that God hates you. It happens to all of us. Notice it. Draw your mind back. If you thought of something critically important, jot it down, save it for later, and focus back on the prayer time at hand. (Stay off social media, email, and anything distracting.)

Read the passage from Nehemiah 1 again.

Ask God to speak to you.

Thank God for every good thing you have that comes to your mind.

Reflect on the chapters of *Favor with Kings* you've read so far. What has been resonating with you? Are you feeling passion starting to burn? Ask God to fan the flame. Tell him you want to focus on the things he wants for you. Ask for clarity.

Consider your history, your hurts, your passion or conviction that is growing. Whom do you feel drawn toward? Whom will you serve?

There are a couple of segments of people to consider: (1) the poor and marginalized; people whom most others in our culture ignore or avoid; and (2) the sphere of influence that we already have; people whom you regularly see, interact with, and relate to.

Serve both. But your passion level might be higher for one or the other.

Write down things you sense, things that become clearer to you, questions you still have.

Ask yourself what it would look like to go "all in." (See *Favor with Kings* chapter 8.)

All in: (1) identifying with and serving others; and (2) total commitment, surrender, and faith.

Ask God for courage, clarity, guidance … and *favor*.

To do whatever you think you need to do, whose blessing do you need? Yes, God's, but assuming you have that, who else's?

In chapter 9, Anderson writes, "God gives favor—but he gives it through authorities."

Whose blessing, backing, belief, support, energy, enthusiasm, or endorsement do you need?

Pray for favor … for blessing.

Come back together as a group.

Additional Questions:

1. How was the prayer experience? Share about your time.

2. What are your next steps?

As you prepare for the next session, catch up on any readings from chapters 6–10 and read as much of chapters 11–15 as possible.

Encourage one another to do the action steps at the end of each chapter. As part of the group experience, you'll also be invited to participate together in one simple action step each week.

Group Action: The prayer experience was your action for this week. Well done. Consider setting aside at least ten minutes a day this week to continue the habit of prayer. (For more resources on prayer and meditation, go to FavorWithKings.com/prayer.)

Close your time together by reading an inspirational quote from *Favor with Kings*.

Note for Next Session: Next time you'll be committing to a service project you'll do as a group. It can be a onetime thing or a vision with ongoing implications. Begin to think about ideas this week.

3. Session Three: Plans

Chapters: 11–15 (*Favor with Kings*)

Overview: Nehemiah prays but doesn't stop at prayer. After praying for God's blessing, he *plans* for God's blessing.

Objective: The goal of this session is to put plans in place. This is the time when things get real. We go beyond ambiguous dreams and passions and start putting plans into action that will serve real people—including people whom your group will serve together over the next few weeks.

Leader Tip: Set the example for the group by having thought through your own plans, personally, so each person can do the same. Then, toward the end of the meeting, shift from personal plans and help the group find the common ground or an obvious need in the community where they can work on a serve project together.

Questions:

1. What's your favorite business or nonprofit organization, and why?

Every great business or organization exists because its leader(s) saw a need in society and believed that they could uniquely meet that need. They became an organization when they got organized and proved the concept.

You don't need to start a company, but you do need to get organized and make plans if anything good is to happen on purpose.

2. Are you confident or unclear about your *purpose* and *passion* and the *people* you might serve? What else do you think you need in order to be more confident?

Group Reading: Nehemiah 2:1–18

> In the month of Nisan in the twentieth year of King Artaxerxes, when wine was brought for him, I took the wine and gave it to the king. I had not been sad in his presence before, so the king asked me, "Why does your face look so sad when you are not ill? This can be nothing but sadness of heart."
>
> I was very much afraid, but I said to the king, "May the king live forever! Why should my face not look sad when the city where my ancestors are buried lies in ruins, and its gates have been destroyed by fire?"
>
> The king said to me, "What is it you want?"
>
> Then I prayed to the God of heaven, and I answered the king, "If it pleases the king and if your servant has found favor in his sight, let him send me to the city in Judah where my ancestors are buried so that I can rebuild it."
>
> Then the king, with the queen sitting beside him, asked me, "How long will your journey take,

and when will you get back?" It pleased the king to send me; so I set a time.

I also said to him, "If it pleases the king, may I have letters to the governors of Trans-Euphrates, so that they will provide me safe-conduct until I arrive in Judah? And may I have a letter to Asaph, keeper of the royal park, so he will give me timber to make beams for the gates of the citadel by the temple and for the city wall and for the residence I will occupy?" And because the gracious hand of my God was on me, the king granted my requests. So I went to the governors of Trans-Euphrates and gave them the king's letters. The king had also sent army officers and cavalry with me.

When Sanballat the Horonite and Tobiah the Ammonite official heard about this, they were very much disturbed that someone had come to promote the welfare of the Israelites.

I went to Jerusalem, and after staying there three days I set out during the night with a few others. I had not told anyone what my God had put in my heart to do for Jerusalem. There were no mounts with me except the one I was riding on.

By night I went out through the Valley Gate toward the Jackal Well and the Dung Gate, examining the walls of Jerusalem, which had been broken down, and its gates, which had been destroyed by fire. Then I moved on toward the Fountain Gate and the King's Pool, but there was not enough room for my mount to get through; so I went up the valley by night, examining the wall. Finally, I turned back and reentered through the Valley Gate. The officials did not know where I had gone or what I was doing, because as yet I had said nothing to the Jews or the priests or nobles or officials or any others who would be doing the work.

Then I said to them, "You see the trouble we are in: Jerusalem lies in ruins, and its gates have been burned with fire. Come, let us rebuild the wall of Jerusalem, and we will no longer be in disgrace." I also told them about the gracious hand of my God on me and what the king had said to me.

Additional Questions:

1. What stands out to you in the passage above?

2. What do you notice about the relationship between Nehemiah and the king of Persia? Why is that personal and working relationship important to the story?

3. If God gave you *favor* with an authority figure who could help you pursue your vision, what might it look like? How could you be preparing for that day now?

4. Considering Nehemiah's example (verses 11–16), what other preparations and plans might help you move toward your vision?

5. As a group, what can you do to serve someone in your community—a person, type of people, or place that needs support?

6. When will you start? Put it on the calendar. (Aim for 100 percent participation, but it might not be possible.)

Examples of serve projects:

- beautification efforts
- mentoring youth
- coaching a team
- caring for children
- engaging with the elderly
- adopting a neighborhood
- serving together at church
- partnering with local nonprofits
- pooling resources (financial and otherwise) to meet a specific need

Our group's serving schedule:

Date: _____

Time: _____

Place: _____

As you prepare for the next session, catch up on any readings from chapters 11–15 and read as much of chapters 16–20 as possible.

Encourage one another to do the action steps at the end of each chapter. As part of the group experience, you'll also be invited to participate together in one simple action step each week.

Group Action: Serve together.

Close your time together with a prayer of alignment—that your plans would be God's plans and that he would bless them.

Note for Next Session: Come prepared next week to talk about your plans. Your vision and plans can (and should) be different from others'. Don't compare or worry about whether your plans are good enough, big enough, or defined enough. That's what this whole process is about. You shouldn't have everything figured out yet. And if you do, you can help others!

4. Session Four: Progress

Chapters: 16–20 (*Favor with Kings*)

Overview: Nehemiah prays and he plans, but plans are worthless without follow-through. Follow-through means taking action, and action leads to *progress.*

Objective: The goal of this session is to move to action.

Leader Tip: Some in your group have projects that are well under way—organized as a business, ministry, or hobby. Others have a vision and plan but have yet to make any progress. Focus each of your members on his or her *next right step.*

Questions:

1. Talk about a time when you committed to a process that seemed long and difficult. How do you view that time now? What were the results?

Group Reading: Nehemiah 2:17–3:15

> Then I said to them, "You see the trouble we are in: Jerusalem lies in ruins, and its gates have been burned with fire. Come, let us rebuild the wall of Jerusalem, and we will no longer be in disgrace." I

also told them about the gracious hand of my God on me and what the king had said to me.

They replied, "Let us start rebuilding." So they began this good work.

But when Sanballat the Horonite, Tobiah the Ammonite official and Geshem the Arab heard about it, they mocked and ridiculed us. "What is this you are doing?" they asked. "Are you rebelling against the king?"

I answered them by saying, "The God of heaven will give us success. We his servants will start rebuilding, but as for you, you have no share in Jerusalem or any claim or historic right to it."

Eliashib the high priest and his fellow priests went to work and rebuilt the Sheep Gate. They dedicated it and set its doors in place, building as far as the Tower of the Hundred, which they dedicated, and as far as the Tower of Hananel. The men of Jericho built the adjoining section, and Zakkur son of Imri built next to them.

The Fish Gate was rebuilt by the sons of Hassenaah. They laid its beams and put its doors and bolts and bars in place. Meremoth son of Uriah, the son of Hakkoz, repaired the next section. Next to him Meshullam son of Berekiah, the son of Meshezabel, made repairs, and next to him Zadok son of Baana also made repairs. The next section was repaired by the men of Tekoa, but their nobles would not put their shoulders to the work under their supervisors.

The Jeshanah Gate was repaired by Joiada son of Paseah and Meshullam son of Besodeiah. They laid its beams and put its doors with their bolts and bars in place. Next to them, repairs were made by men from Gibeon and Mizpah—Melatiah of Gibeon and Jadon of Meronoth—places under the authority of the governor of Trans-Euphrates. Uzziel son of Harhaiah, one of the goldsmiths, repaired the next section; and Hananiah, one of the perfume-makers, made repairs next to that. They restored Jerusalem as far as the Broad Wall. Rephaiah son of Hur, ruler of a half-district of Jerusalem, repaired the next section. Adjoining this, Jedaiah son of Harumaph made repairs opposite his house, and Hattush son of Hashabneiah made repairs next to him. Malkijah son of Harim and Hasshub son of Pahath-Moab repaired another section and the Tower of the Ovens. Shallum son of Hallohesh, ruler of a half-district of Jerusalem, repaired the next section with the help of his daughters.

The Valley Gate was repaired by Hanun and the residents of Zanoah. They rebuilt it and put its doors with their bolts and bars in place. They also repaired a thousand cubits of the wall as far as the Dung Gate.

The Dung Gate was repaired by Malkijah son of Rekab, ruler of the district of Beth Hakkerem. He rebuilt it and put its doors with their bolts and bars in place.

The Fountain Gate was repaired by Shallun son of Kol-Hozeh, ruler of the district of Mizpah. He rebuilt it, roofing it over and putting its doors and bolts and bars in place. He also repaired the wall of the Pool of Siloam, by the King's Garden, as far as the steps going down from the City of David.

Additional Questions:

1. What stands out to you in the passage above? Beyond all the crazy names, what do you see?

2. What does Nehemiah do to "spark" the change?

3. What do you notice about the "system" Nehemiah puts in place for the construction of the gates?

4. What systems, habits, or routines do you currently use to get things done? What new ones might you need to accomplish the vision?

5. Are there any small wins or breakthroughs that can be celebrated?

6. If you've already done your group serve project, what did you learn? (If not, refer back to your serve schedule.)

As you prepare for the next session, catch up on any readings from chapters 16–20 and read as much of chapters 21–25 as possible.

Encourage one another to do the action steps at the end of each chapter. As part of the group experience, you'll also be invited to participate together in one simple action step each week.

Group Action: Follow up from your group serve outing. Either do the serve project (if you haven't yet) or brainstorm how your group can continue to serve together with some kind of rhythm—monthly, quarterly, etc.

Close your time together with a prayer for courage and clarity on your next right step.

Note for Next Session: Come prepared next week to talk about your progress. Any step—small or large—will be celebrated and built upon.

5. Session Five: Persistence and perseverance

Chapters: 21–25 (*Favor with Kings*)

Overview: Progress requires putting people to work in their areas of passion and then persisting in the face of opposition.

Objective: Encourage one another to work together with people and endure through pain to see their vision become a reality.

Leader Tip: It's not likely that many in your group will yet be to the point of conflict or heavy opposition. But those days are coming. Refer back to past experiences and familiar stories, encouraging one another for the days ahead.

Question:

Talk about your favorite story of a hero persevering through great difficulty.

Group Reading: Nehemiah 3:28–4:9

> Above the Horse Gate, the priests made repairs, each in front of his own house. Next to them, Zadok son of Immer made repairs opposite his house. Next to him, Shemaiah son of Shekaniah, the guard at the East Gate, made repairs. Next to him, Hananiah son of Shelemiah, and Hanun,

the sixth son of Zalaph, repaired another section. Next to them, Meshullam son of Berekiah made repairs opposite his living quarters. Next to him, Malkijah, one of the goldsmiths, made repairs as far as the house of the temple servants and the merchants, opposite the Inspection Gate, and as far as the room above the corner; and between the room above the corner and the Sheep Gate the goldsmiths and merchants made repairs.

When Sanballat heard that we were rebuilding the wall, he became angry and was greatly incensed. He ridiculed the Jews, and in the presence of his associates and the army of Samaria, he said, "What are those feeble Jews doing? Will they restore their wall? Will they offer sacrifices? Will they finish in a day? Can they bring the stones back to life from those heaps of rubble—burned as they are?"

Tobiah the Ammonite, who was at his side, said, "What they are building—even a fox climbing up on it would break down their wall of stones!"

Hear us, our God, for we are despised. Turn their insults back on their own heads. Give them over as plunder in a land of captivity. Do not cover up their guilt or blot out their sins from your sight, for they have thrown insults in the face of the builders.

So we rebuilt the wall till all of it reached half its height, for the people worked with all their heart.

But when Sanballat, Tobiah, the Arabs, the Ammonites and the people of Ashdod heard that the repairs to Jerusalem's walls had gone ahead and that the gaps were being closed, they were very angry. They all plotted together to come and fight against Jerusalem and stir up trouble against it. But we prayed to our God and posted a guard day and night to meet this threat.

Additional Questions:

1. What stands out to you in the passage above?

2. What is Nehemiah's genius delegation strategy? Why do you think he assigns the work the way he does?

3. Which people or groups already have a passion connected to your vision or a stake in the desired outcome? How can you engage them? (Think about your personal vision and the group project, if relevant.)

4. What kind of opposition have you experienced, or do you expect to encounter, on your journey?

5. What does Nehemiah do in the face of serious threats? What can you learn from his actions?

6. How can you support one another knowing that opposition is inevitable when you're on a mission from God?

7. What does Os Guinness's question, "Is the revolution still on?" (*Favor with Kings*, chapter 25) mean to you?

As you prepare for the next session, catch up on any readings from chapters 21–25 and read as much of chapters 25–30 as possible.

Encourage one another to do the action steps at the end of each chapter. As part of the group experience, you'll also be invited to participate together in one simple action step each week.

Group Action: Call one person in your group this week and encourage him or her. Ask your own form of the question, "Is the revolution still on?"

Close your time together with a prayer acknowledging that while opposition is inevitable, good will triumph over evil in the end.

Note for Next Session: The next session is the sixth and final (official) discussion in the *Favor with Kings* study. Obviously, your group is encouraged to continue meeting, but now is a great time to plan a "fun" night. After your sixth and final meeting, gather together at least once more just to celebrate what God did in your six weeks together. Put the date on the calendar now. Don't do anything too serious. Eat, play, laugh, and enjoy the time together.

6. Session Six: Power

Chapters: 26–30 (*Favor with Kings*)

Overview: Your project is a mission from God. It's not for you. It's bigger than you.

Objective: Begin with the end in mind. Consider what it will look like to lead others with integrity and leave a legacy.

Leader Tip: It's not likely that many in your group will yet be to the point of handing off their project, ministry, or business. However, the goal is to begin with the end in mind. Take opportunities to gently remind one another that this is God's work happening through us, but it is not exclusively *for* us. We're doing what we're doing for others. And that is what produces fulfillment in us.

Question:

Discuss a time when you received benefits because of the efforts, position, or resources of someone else.

Group Reading: Nehemiah 5

> Now the men and their wives raised a great outcry against their fellow Jews. Some were saying, "We and our sons and daughters are numerous; in order for us to eat and stay alive, we must get grain."

Others were saying, "We are mortgaging our fields, our vineyards and our homes to get grain during the famine."

Still others were saying, "We have had to borrow money to pay the king's tax on our fields and vineyards. Although we are of the same flesh and blood as our fellow Jews and though our children are as good as theirs, yet we have to subject our sons and daughters to slavery. Some of our daughters have already been enslaved, but we are powerless, because our fields and our vineyards belong to others."

When I heard their outcry and these charges, I was very angry. I pondered them in my mind and then accused the nobles and officials. I told them, "You are charging your own people interest!" So I called together a large meeting to deal with them and said: "As far as possible, we have bought back our fellow Jews who were sold to the Gentiles. Now you are selling your own people, only for them to be sold back to us!" They kept quiet, because they could find nothing to say.

So I continued, "What you are doing is not right. Shouldn't you walk in the fear of our God to avoid the reproach of our Gentile enemies? I and my brothers and my men are also lending the people money and grain. But let us stop charging interest! Give back to them immediately their fields, vineyards, olive groves and houses, and also the interest you are charging them—one percent of the money, grain, new wine and olive oil."

"We will give it back," they said. "And we will not demand anything more from them. We will do as you say."

Then I summoned the priests and made the nobles and officials take an oath to do what they had promised. I also shook out the folds of my robe and said, "In this way may God shake out of their house and possessions anyone who does not keep this promise. So may such a person be shaken out and emptied!"

At this the whole assembly said, "Amen," and praised the Lord. And the people did as they had promised.

Moreover, from the twentieth year of King Artaxerxes, when I was appointed to be their governor in the land of Judah, until his thirty-second year—twelve years—neither I nor my brothers ate the food allotted to the governor. But the earlier governors—those preceding me—placed a heavy burden on the people and took forty shekels of silver from them in addition to food and wine. Their assistants also lorded it over the people. But out of reverence for God I did not act like that. Instead, I devoted myself to the work on this wall. All my men were assembled there for the work; we did not acquire any land.

Furthermore, a hundred and fifty Jews and officials ate at my table, as well as those who came to us from the surrounding nations. Each day one ox, six choice sheep and some poultry were prepared for me, and every ten days an abundant supply of wine of all kinds. In spite of all this, I never demanded the food allotted to the governor, because the demands were heavy on these people.

Remember me with favor, my God, for all I have done for these people.

Additional Questions:

1. What stands out to you in the passage above?

2. How are some people exploiting others? What is Nehemiah's response?

3. As Anderson says, "The project has always been about the people." When have you seen people taken advantage of or exploited?

4. Nehemiah communicates that it's a new day—there is a *new normal*—and the behavior in question is no longer acceptable. What kind of "new normal" are you hoping to see?

5. What do you think of Nehemiah's example of sacrifice and integrity in this passage? What present-day parallels can you draw?

6. What commitment are you willing to make to the cause, project, or vision? What decision can you make today that will serve the greater good in the future?

Now is a good time to note any additional highlights, quotes, or questions you have from your reading of *Favor with Kings*.

Encourage one another to *continue* to do the action steps at the end of each chapter and to persevere on your mission from God.

Read the rest of Nehemiah's memoirs on your own time. Reflect on the inspiration and insights you gained from *Favor with Kings*. Follow through on decisions you made through this process. You might find it helpful to choose one person to intentionally follow up with for mutual encouragement over the next few months.

Group Action: Answer the following questions together:

- Will our group continue to meet together?
- If so, on what rhythm (weekly, every other week …)? What day and time?
- How will we continue to serve together?
- How will we commit to encouraging one another's projects?

Close your time together with a prayer asking for God's ongoing blessing and favor in your lives.

Note for Next Steps: Who else needs the inspiration of *Favor with Kings?* Send them a book. (Reviews on Amazon.com are also helpful.)

Refer to your book regularly on your journey to help you stay the course.

Visit FavorWithKings.com for additional resources and to connect with Caleb Anderson.

May God bless you, and may he bless others through you.

FavorWithKings.com

FOR PASTORS

Being a pastor myself, I have created additional resources for you to use as you interact with this book. You'll find them at FavorWithKings.com.

Consider doing a six-week church-wide campaign using *Favor with Kings* as a catalytic tool in your church. By "campaign" I mean: sermon, small groups, and daily readings all aligned and leveraged for mass participation and maximum impact in your congregation.

At Mariners Church, we did a six-week series based on the story of Nehemiah and the content of *Favor with Kings*. Everything you need in order to do something similar can be found at:

FavorWithKings.com/pastor

I took this photo with my iPhone in November 2015 at the base of
the Temple Mount. Random tourist for scale.

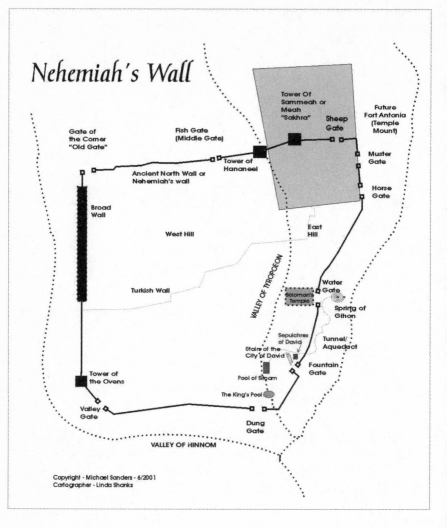

NOTES

1. Read Genesis 1, but not as a bedtime story. Read it like it's your genesis.

2. Matthew 22:36–40.

3. Matthew 20:20–28.

4. Romans 8:28.

5. 2 Chronicles 36:18–20.

6. Ezra 4.

7. If you're not sure you've adequately dealt with tragedy, loss, and pain in your life, counseling is a great place to start. Counseling helps you look back so you can move forward.

8. LeBron James, interview by Lee Jenkins, in LeBron James, "I'm Coming Home," *Sports Illustrated*, July 11, 2014, http://www.si.com/nba/2014/07/11/lebron-james -cleveland-cavaliers.

9. Book of Esther.

10. Esther 4:13–14.

11. "Truth" is a general reference to Scripture, not that the Bible contains all the truth in existence, but it's the right place to start.

12. See the books of Matthew, Mark, Luke, and John. If you don't know anything about Jesus or the Bible, don't worry. Some of it is in you—you just haven't realized it was from Jesus. Plus, you can start with this next way to hear from God and work your way back.

13. Proverbs 12:15 NIV.

14. "Who Inspires Tony Robbins?," Success.com, December 4, 2014, www.success
.com/article/who-inspires-tony-robbins#sthash.Y1uVtRcG.dpuf.

15. My book *My Near Death Experiment* explores the life lessons we can learn from
others without having to make the same mistakes—making the most of our
lives without the disasters.

16. Proverbs 8; Proverbs 3–4; and James 1:5, respectively.

17. Simon Sinek, "How Great Leaders Inspire Action," TEDxPuget Sound, September
2009, http://www.ted.com/talks/simon_sinek_how_great_leaders_inspire_action.

18. The idea of "what matters most" is addressed in much more detail in *My Near
Death Experiment.*

19. 2 Corinthians 5:13 NIV.

20. I'm sure there are exceptions, but adding the word *almost* to the front of this
sentence would be lame.

21. Daniel 4:25.

22. Ephesians 6:12.

23. Psalm 37:4.

24. Benjamin Gleisser, "Managing to Win," *UNLV Magazine* 22, no. 1 (Spring 2014): 32,
https://issuu.com/university.of.nevada.las.vegas/docs/unlvmagazinespring2014.

25. Mark 10:46–52; Luke 18:35–42.

26. Proverbs 16:9.

27. Nehemiah 2:4–5.

28. Joshua 3.

29. Doris Kearns Goodwin, *Team of Rivals: The Political Genius of Abraham Lincoln*
(New York: Simon and Schuster, 2005).

30. Matthew 25:40.

31. 2 Samuel 23.

32. Ecclesiastes 4:9–10, see also verses 11–12.

33. Psalm 23:4.

34. Her website is AmberAndersonDesign.com.

35. Nehemiah 2:17–18.

36. Genesis 1:27.

37. Proverbs 18:21 CEV.

38. Matthew 17:20.

39. Romans 8:31.

40. Perhaps not perfectly in context, but I still think Philippians 1:6 is relevant.

41. Nehemiah 2:18.

42. I don't know where I first read this story, but it is credited to David Mills, 2012.

43. Matthew 19:26.

44. Revelation 21:5.

45. Romans 8:28 NCV.

46. *Chewables* is now the title of my podcast. The book was later republished under the name *40 Days to a New You*.

47. Romans 8:28.

48. See image in appendix.

49. I'm paraphrasing Joshua 6.

50. The Heath brothers' book is called *Switch*.

51. Thomas J. Peters and Robert H. Waterman, *In Search of Excellence* (New York: Harper and Row, 1982), 122.

52. Numbers 13.

53. Most clearly Sanballat of the Horonites and Tobiah of the Ammonites were driven from the Promised Land.

54. Nehemiah 4:1–2.

55. Nehemiah 4:11.

56. Nehemiah 4:13–14, 16.

57. John 16:33.

58. Ephesians 6:12.

59. Nehemiah 4:5.

60. Nehemiah 4:10.

61. "Eleven Facts about Human Trafficking," DoSomething.org, accessed May 3, 2016, www.dosomething.org/us/facts/11-facts-about-human-trafficking.

62. Nehemiah 4:14.

63. Nehemiah 4:12.

64. Philippians 1:6.

65. Deuteronomy 31:6, 8; Hebrews 13:5; Joshua 1:5.

66. Matthew 28:20.

67. Matthew 22:37–40.

68. 1 Timothy 6:12.

69. "Let the little children come to me … The kingdom of heaven belongs to such as these" (Matthew 19:14).

70. One of my good friends on my staff is named Jairus—the only one I know. This story is found in Luke 8.

71. Luke 8:45–46.

72. Mark 9:35.

73. Psalm 37:5.

74. Nehemiah 5:18.

75. Mark 8:36.

76. Nehemiah 5:19.

77. Matthew 6:20–29.

78. Matthew 10:39; 16:25.

79. Hebrews 11:1.

80. Nehemiah 6:14.

81. Hebrews 12:1.

82. Jesus came first to his people—the Jews—but came to save all people.

83. Nehemiah 6:15–16.

84. Nehemiah 4:6.

85. Nehemiah 7.

86. Nehemiah 8:1–3.

87. Nehemiah 8:10.

88. Nehemiah 5:17.

89. Nehemiah 7:2.

90. Matthew 7:6.

91. Nehemiah 8:10.

BIBLE CREDITS